OUTSIDE AGITATOR

OUTSIDE AGITATOR

the CIVIL RIGHTS STRUGGLE *of* CLEVELAND SELLERS JR.

ADAM PARKER

HUB CITY PRESS

SPARTANBURG, SC

Copyright © 2018 Adam Parker

Photo credits:
122, 125, 132, 135: Avery Institute of Afro-American History of Culture
134: Charlotte Observer
127, 132, 128: Bob Fitch Photography Archive,
Department of Special Collections, Standford University Library
135: Mark Stetler, Camera Works Photography
Other photos, courtesy of Cleveland Sellers Jr.

Book Design: Kate McMullen
Cover design: Meg Reid
Cover photo: Mark Stetler, Camera Works Photography
Printed in Dallas, TX by Versa Printing

TEXT Janson Text LT Pro 11.2/16.2

Library of Congress Cataloging-in-Publication Data

Names: Parker, Adam, 1965- author.
Title: Outside agitator : the civil rights struggle of Cleveland Sellers Jr.
/ Adam Parker.
Other titles: Civil rights struggle of Cleveland Sellers Jr.
Description: Spartanburg, SC : Hub City Press, [2018]
Identifiers: LCCN 2018019633 | ISBN 9781938235450
Subjects: LCSH: Sellers, Cleveland, 1944- | Student Nonviolent Coordinating
Committee (U.S.)--Biography. | African American civil rights
workers--Biography. | Civil rights workers--Southern States--Biography.
African Americans--Civil rights--Southern States. | Civil rights
movements--Southern States--History--20th century. | Orangeburg Massacre,
Orangeburg, S.C., 1968. | Voorhees College--Biography. | Denmark
(S.C.)--Biography. | Southern States--Race relations.
Classification: LCC E185.61 .P24 2018 | DDC 323.092 [B] --dc23
LC record available at https://lccn.loc.gov/2018019633

186 W. Main Street
Spartanburg, SC 29306
1.864.577.9349
www.hubcity.org

TABLE OF CONTENTS

PROLOGUE

CLEVELAND SELLERS JR. is soft-spoken, though his words typically contain some urgency and are informed by a deep intelligence. He has taken time to process his many years of activism, reconciling personal history with larger political and social trends, so he talks about his past professorially. His broad smile and expressions of friendship belie a ferocity fueled not by a raging heat but by a blue flame within that seems impossible to extinguish, even as he mellows with age. His easy manner obscures a certain determination, a drive to get things done, to explain the facts and make the point, to put things in order. He is a steady force, the reliable one who observes as much as he acts and recognizes when something's amiss.

Patience should be his middle name. He affirms an interlocutor's observations or small epiphanies with the encouraging air of a grandfather who long ago came to terms with an imperfect world but enjoys it when a younger person recognizes the truisms of injustice. He is, at heart, a teacher. He does not seek the spotlight; he is content behind the scenes. These character traits are partly responsible for the subdued charisma he exudes and the leadership status he easily achieves whatever the endeavor. These traits are informed by years of internalized stress that has resulted in some psychological and physical wear and tear and, possibly, has contributed to heart problems he is experiencing late in his life.

As a young man—tall and lean, quiet, good-looking, a bit severe—he tended to prefer the second row. He was well known within the Student Nonviolent Coordinating Committee (SNCC), but hardly known outside of it—that is, until 1967 when he refused the draft and made headlines. Like most everyone involved in the civil rights movement, he changed significantly over the course of the 1960s, from an eager, clean-cut activist to a Black Power proponent dressed in a dashiki and wearing his hair in an afro. While most sensible young people tended to avoid becoming embroiled in racial conflicts, Sellers was among the few who ran headlong into the fray. He had a soldier's ability to compartmentalize the issues and the dangers, and he tended to focus first on the former. It was only later, when he was reflecting on what happened, that Sellers would come to appreciate the perils to which he had subjected himself. In this way the stress of political activism accumulated within him.

The SNCC activist who organized voter drives in Mississippi, gathered evidence of discrimination and fraud in order to challenge the Democratic Party's exclusionary racial policies, obsessed about SNCC's inventory of vehicles and pushed students to delve into black identity issues became a significant figure on the government's list of threatening black militants. By the mid-1960s, he was a target of the FBI's covert COINTELPRO operation whose purpose was to infiltrate and delegitimize black organizations and to marginalize—and sometimes to spur the removal of—black leaders. On February 8, 1968, Sellers was attempting to convince protesting students at South Carolina State College to withdraw from a volatile confrontation with state troopers, police, sheriff's deputies, National Guardsmen and FBI agents when the riot guns went off. The SNCC activist was the scapegoat and the only person to serve time in jail for what became known as the Orangeburg Massacre. The year 2018 marks the 50th anniversary of that tragic event in which three black students were killed and at least 28 wounded. It was the first-ever campus shooting in the United States involving law enforcement and one of the most violent episodes of the civil rights movement. It challenged the myth of South Carolina moderation and accommodation, and it produced the state's deepest racial wound, one that still has not fully healed. Yet the Orangeburg Massacre was initially misrepresented by state officials and the press, and it was soon overshadowed entirely by another campus shooting in 1970, this time affecting white students protesting the Vietnam War at Kent State University. Since the Orangeburg catastrophe, Sellers has borne the labels of "scapegoat" and "outside agitator," and for decades was burdened by the criminal charges levied against him. He has spent the last 50 years striving to overcome an injustice that few today know anything about.

In the beginning Sellers was a foot soldier, then a bureaucrat. For years he remained in the shadow of Stokely Carmichael, the brilliant firebrand and dynamic leader on whom the spotlight was focused, for good and ill. But Sellers, too, was a vocal critic of the Vietnam War and an advocate of Black Power. He was an educator who rose within SNCC's ranks and, eventually, within academia to advance his goals. It was many such committed people who made the movement possible and ensured its halting successes. Big speeches and TV appearances are important, to be sure, but the generals and majors cannot win a war without the sergeants and infantrymen. Excellent volumes have been published on Martin Luther King Jr., Stokely Carmichael and Malcolm X, but the movement includes many other remarkable figures and historically significant events that have yet to be fully explored. As the history of America's civil rights movement continues to be written, more and more books are devoted to fleshing out the facts, broadening the cast of characters, filling in the blanks, introducing nuances, dispelling old assumptions and giving credit where credit is due. Sellers is one of the leaders whose fascinating life story deserves to be widely shared. Pieces of this story have appeared elsewhere, most notably in his own autobiography, *River of No Return: An Autobiography of a Black Militant and the Life and Death of SNCC* (William Morrow, 1973), and in two important volumes about the campus shooting at South Carolina State and its impacts, an updated version of *The Orangeburg Massacre* by Jack Bass and Jack Nelson (Mercer University Press, 1996), and *Blood and Bone: Truth and Reconciliation in a Southern Town* by Jack Shuler (University of South Carolina Press, 2012).

Outside Agitator recounts Sellers' life in full, from his childhood in the tiny rural town of Denmark, through his years of civil rights activism and decades of self-imposed exile in Greensboro, North Carolina, to his eventual academic challenges and triumphs. It all began for Sellers in 1955, when he was 10. That's when he learned about the brutal murder of Emmett Till, a 14-year-old Chicago native visiting relatives in Mississippi. Four years later, Sellers, inspired by the Greensboro sit-ins, helped organize a lunch counter protest in Denmark. He could not have known in 1959 that, by virtue of his birth date, hometown, quietly charismatic personality and family's social status, he would become a determined and prominent agent for change in the 1960s, a victim of officially sanctioned brutality and, eventually, an educator who helped transform the way academia addressed matters of race, history and society. All he knew in the first 16 years since his birth on November 8, 1944, was that he had entered a decidedly segregated world, and that to be black in this world meant to fend for oneself.

Cleveland Sellers helped shape our history. He propelled himself into the great, unstoppable ocean current that circumnavigates the globe, albeit in a roundabout way, enriching regional waters with necessary nutrients, though he did not avoid all the shipwrecks. He rode the waves of progress, sometimes tumbling into the roiling surf. His experiences teach us not only about the civil rights movement, but about America and its values, about the ways its leaders have tried to disrupt the current, about the competing forces at play that turn some into martyrs and others into heroes. Sellers' life-defining moment—the Orangeburg Massacre—is also one of *our* defining moments, though too few understand what happened and what it meant for our democracy.

We can learn much from Sellers and his ability to navigate a treacherous current with skill. He shows us what perseverance means, and what confrontation can achieve and what it can destroy. Most of all, Sellers shows us that progress is determined not only by the inexorable turn of the Earth and swirl of its seas, but by the actions of those who insist on fighting for social and economic justice. A better world is achievable, if we want it badly enough.

1

CHILDHOOD IN DENMARK

DRIVING INTO DENMARK today along South Carolina Highway 70, one sees but a shell of the bustling small Bamberg County town that once epitomized life in the South. J.J.'s Automotive Repair claims the intersection with Carolina Highway, the main drag that runs through the center of town, though its dilapidated state and lack of activity is an indicator of Denmark's decline. Nice houses, well maintained with their manicured yards, are nestled among tall pines and cornfields on the outskirts of town. Historically, this is where the whites live; blacks mostly occupy less noble structures on the south side of Denmark and across the railroad tracks to the west. Clearly, there are still some who prefer this rural lifestyle, who remain in their family homes and who satisfy their material needs by driving 23 miles east to Orangeburg, or winding their way to Columbia, the state's capital, 50 miles to the north.

In Denmark, population 3,000, only a handful of the stores on Carolina Highway are open today. An antique shop attracts a few customers; an art gallery founded by the late Jim Harrison (the pride of the town) remains open but without the steady customer base that once came to meet the artist. The Dane Theater, a movie house built in the 1940s, has been renovated into a cultural center. The fire department has a relatively new building. A park has been named in honor of Harrison, the artist. But the lights remain off inside many of the shops. After decades of economic and social stagnation, and a diminishing middle class, young people have mostly abandoned the town to get educated in Columbia or Charleston or elsewhere, and they have stayed away in their attempts to find work. The population of this hamlet has dropped nearly 25 percent since 1990. It is difficult to imagine—to admit—that during the Jim Crow era this area pulsated with life. At one time Denmark was home to a Coca-Cola bottling plant, a pickle plant, a furniture manufacturer. It was a hub for three train lines: the Atlantic Coast Service, Seaboard Coast Line and Southern Railway.

Cleveland Sellers, known to his family and friends as Cleve, was born here on November 8, 1944. Walking through the town, he points to the motel his father opened in 1969. Now closed, it was the first black-owned motel in Denmark. Later converted into apartments, the building sits next to Cleve's childhood home at 432 Frederick Street, a modest ranch surrounded by trees, where he was raised, along with his older sister. He cruises slowly up Carolina Highway, a melancholy expression belying his matter-of-fact descriptions of what happened here 60 years ago. Sellers is good at explaining things, his discursive style honed over the years thanks to his political activism and academic experience. He remembers the movie theater, the afternoon activities, the solidarity among blacks, the otherness of whites. He recalls episodes from his childhood, the friends he played with, the pony he rode and his parents, who were well-informed, loving and protective.

CLEVE'S FATHER, Cleveland Sellers Sr., was among Denmark's enterprising blacks during the days of segregation. He operated a taxi business, driving passengers between South Carolina and New York and people who were denied access to public transportation. For a spell he shuttled a blind doctor to and from patients scattered about the county. He ran a cafe. He rented properties. He even raised cattle at one point. The elder Sellers was a small-town businessman in a place defined by its rural surroundings. He had graduated from Voorhees High School, an impressive accomplishment at the time.

The Southern Homestead Act of 1866 gave rise to the South Carolina Land Commission, formed in 1868, which bought large plantations from white owners no longer able to manage them profitably and divided the land into small parcels, making it possible for poor blacks and whites, including some in Bamberg County, to purchase family farms at low prices. This created a new class of farmers, many of whom helped set the stage for the entrepreneurship of Sellers Sr. and other enterprising black men. In 1868-1879, the Land Commission sold farmland to 14,000 African-American families.

Thus an economy dominated by agriculture, and later manufacturing, provided subsistence to those who inherited the legacy of slavery and who managed to achieve self-sufficiency both despite and because of segregation. The black side of town was clearly defined and featured black-owned businesses, schools, churches and social groups. Sellers' parents functioned almost entirely within this community. They married late, on March 23, 1941. Pauline Taggart, born in McCormick County, was 37; Cleveland Sellers Sr., born in Denmark, was 31. Both were success-minded and enterprising. Pauline, the better educated of the two, had received her Bachelor of Science degree in home economics from State Agricultural and Mechanical College (which later would become South Carolina State University), the first black school of higher education supported by the state. She pursued graduate studies at the Hampton Institute (now Hampton University) in Virginia, though she did not earn a degree there. After her schooling, she returned to South Carolina and became a public school teacher, first at the Brewer Normal School in Greenwood, then at Emmett Scott High School in Rock Hill, then in the Columbia system, eventually ending up back in Denmark at Voorhees Normal and Industrial Institute, a school for young black students. By the time her two children were born, she was a dietician and teacher at the adjacent Area Trade School (now Denmark Technical College). One of seven sisters, she was a member of the AME church, NAACP and American Association of University Women. She was also associated with St. Philip's Chapel, the local Episcopal church for blacks on the campus of Voorhees. "My mom was a very kind person, and she was concerned about the community 24/7," Sellers said. "She worked, so she had to put that kind of focus and activity on the weekends when she could squeeze it in." Despite her divided attention, she was very nurturing. "I'd have to say I was a mother's boy and grew up under her wing." Early on, Sellers learned valuable lessons from his mother that would influence his later activism and professional career: "To have a successful plan you have to be organized." And to execute that plan well you have to have a strong work ethic and an ability to manage many activities at once, he said.

At school, Cleve Sellers sometimes would share his lunch with friends too poor to bring food every day. When his mother found out, she began to prepare extra lunches for those kids, and her discovery of certain families in need prompted her to reach out. "She decided to take a family on," Sellers recalled. She would gather up leftovers from the trade school cafeteria and deliver them. Cleve was expected to help. The precariousness of poverty became glaringly evident when, later, a close friend left Denmark to pick tobacco on a farm in Connecticut and decided not to return. The friend ended up in New York City, where he died, probably of a drug overdose, Sellers said. His absence, and then his death, hit Cleve hard, teaching him his first lessons of loss.

Cleveland Sellers Sr. put his entrepreneurial skills to work starting in 1936. He launched the taxi service, opened the restaurant and ran the motel, each bearing his name. His success led to the purchase of land and homes that he rented or sold for a profit. "By the time Cleve was a teenager, his father owned more than 20 homes and had become a leader in Denmark's black community," writes Charles Marsh in his book *God's Long Summer*. Sellers Sr. was a strong proponent of the Booker T. Washington school of self-reliance: Only hard work can lead to a better lot in life. He joined the military, becoming an army technician fourth grade, serving in World War II and receiving a campaign medal. "He was always an entrepreneur, and that came from the industrial education that was part of Voorhees High School," his son said. "It was all about building within the framework of what you had available to you."

That framework, restricted by Jim Crow, did not stop the elder Sellers from pursuing all sorts of projects. "A lot of the time he was just busy working on one thing or another," Sellers Jr. said. In the 1940s and 1950s, when Cleveland Sellers Sr. operated his popular little restaurant and juke joint called Sellers Cafe, blacks in Denmark (for reasons of necessity) were relatively independent. The road into the town that passed Voorhees High School was dominated by small black-owned farms, and closer to the center of town, a number of black merchants catered exclusively to other blacks. The small town was not notably acrimonious during this period. It cannot be said that race relations were *bad*. Race relations were essentially non-existent; whites and blacks mingled hardly at all. Segregation was in force, and broadly accepted without very much dissent. Jim Campbell, a Charleston resident who was a student at Voorhees High School in the early 1950s, remembered the authoritative role Sellers Sr. played in the community. "We would sneak away and walk that mile to Denmark at night, down the road past these cottages where a number of African-American farm families lived, and go to Cleve Sellers' place," Campbell recalled. "It was the only place in town." There, young people would gather to socialize, dance to juke box music and eat typical Southern fare—fried chicken and fish, rice, fresh vegetables. Always there was Cleveland Sellers Sr. keeping an eye on everyone. "And he would always encourage us to be careful not to overdo it," Campbell said. "He was like a community mentor. That's all I knew about him."

Interaction with whites during this long period of segregation was practically nil. "The only white folks we saw—that I can remember seeing—were people, a group of three, who would come annually to visit the school, Voorhees," Campbell said. "I guess they were fundraisers or benefactors in some way. But we would get cleaned up, they would sit down front, we would meet in the auditorium and the choir would sing for them."

The Sellers family was part of an enclave that prioritized education. Pauline Sellers paid attention to politics, her son said. They spoke freely about the 1954 *Brown v. Board of Education* decision and the 1955 Montgomery Bus Boycott. They consulted magazines and periodicals such as the Chicago Defender, Ebony, Jet and the Norfolk Journal and Guide. At school, young students were uninhibited, discussing the latest developments and their implications. The bus boycott seemed especially significant: "We saw that African Americans began to move away from legalism as a tactic toward direct action," Sellers said.

His older sister, Gwendolyn Sellers Parker, called the Denmark of her youth "a nice little town" that boasted a solid, if small, black middle class: "We had our own community. We had our own doctors and dentists. And we had Voorhees High School and Junior College. So, we had our professors. We had, at that time it was called Denmark Area Trade School, which is Denmark Technical College today. The people who taught those courses were either very skilled in what they taught or they had college degrees. And everybody who taught at Voorhees [High] had college degrees."

FOR THE TOWN'S African-American residents, life in Denmark revolved around church and school, and Voorhees—initially a high school and later a college—was the focus of much of the activity. Voorhees' founder, Elizabeth Evelyn Wright, advanced the idea, popular at the turn of the 20th century during Jim Crow, that self-sufficiency was essential to survival and accomplished through educational systems that were operated and controlled by blacks. (That many of the early trade schools, "normal" schools and other institutions were funded in part by white abolitionists, civil rights advocates and church officials was a necessary contradiction in the quest for self-determination among the first generations of former slaves.) Called Denmark Industrial School upon its founding in 1897, the institution acquired its current name at the turn of the century when New Jersey philanthropist Ralph Voorhees and his wife donated $5,000 to buy land and erect the first building.

Voorhees High School followed in 1902 with Wright as its first principal. Denmark had no public high school for blacks. Voorhees High was a private institution and struggled to educate the children of black farmers and merchants in the area, including Sellers Sr. and his son. Other students, from Savannah, New York City, North Carolina or small towns in South Carolina, were sent by their parents to Voorhees, which functioned as a boarding school. The dynamic student body with its mix of rural and urban experiences, the committed teachers and insular nature of the school made it a hotbed of learning and college prep.

"We had the private boarding students. We had the city students. Then we had the junior college students," Sellers' sister Gwen Parker said. "The freshmen and sophomores who graduated went on, a lot of them, to four-year colleges and graduated. Our high school experience was totally different from the average, because they brought in what they called lyceum programs—cultural activities. They brought in plays and groups from New York. And so we got a different kind of experience, as opposed to a kid who was just going to high school." There was also a robust sports program that included basketball and football, she said. Voorhees, and other black schools that included a junior college, often evolved during the middle part of the 20th century into regular four-year accredited colleges.

The quasi-college environment offered students a rigorous education and likely accounted for the large numbers that went on to pursue degrees, Parker said. Because of the presence of junior college students, Voorhees High School students were exposed to advanced thinking on a variety of topics, to quality sports and to a library that included college-level materials. In 1922, the president of Voorhees Normal School, Joshua Blanton, forged an agreement with The Episcopal Church and its American Church Institute for Negroes (now defunct). The church took an active role in helping to improve the lives of Southern blacks through education and other programs. The affiliation has persisted over the years, though today very little funding comes from the church. On campus is St. Philip's Chapel where students attended twice-weekly services and the community's population of black Episcopalians worshipped. (Whites attended Christ Church on Carolina Highway.)

As a teacher at the trade school on campus, Pauline Sellers witnessed the establishment of St. Philip's Chapel in 1935 and attended services there, even if she never abandoned Bethel AME Church. As a boy, Cleveland Sellers was an acolyte at St. Philip's, soon assisting the Reverend Henry Grant under the steep gable roof and within the thick brick walls. "I must have spent 15 or 16 years as an acolyte," he recalled. "I was going to [St. Philip's]church because my mother was still very active in the women's auxiliaries." Two of the other child acolytes were Marshall and Matthew Jones, the sons of the rector. A decade or so later, when Sellers was embroiled in the civil rights movement, he would encounter the brothers again: they had become Freedom Singers, who traveled throughout the country singing protest songs and building support for the movement. Sellers literally grew up in the small Episcopal parish, spending much of his childhood in a robe and sash. Grant was an activist priest, merging theology with social concerns in the tradition of Southern black preachers. "I admired Grant so much, I thought about the priesthood," Sellers said. "I was enthralled by him, his wisdom, his passion."

Grant was focused on the children in the church. He took them to an Episcopal camp and made himself available if any of his young parishioners had a problem. After five years, Grant was pressured to leave, probably because of a divorce that didn't sit well with the church. By that time, he had instilled in the young acolyte an uneasy notion that his own future would include struggle and pressure. (Grant, it should be noted, would move to Charleston and become a prominent figure in that city's civil rights struggle. He pastored a church in the mostly black East Side neighborhood, shuttled and sheltered protestors and became a behind-the-scenes advocate for the equal treatment of black health care workers during the 1969 Hospital Strike.)

YOUNG SELLERS WAS a product of middle-class values. He liked Roy Rogers and Trigger; he read about Tarzan and the Lone Ranger. He bought comic books such as Adventure Comics' "Superboy" and "Batman." He read Lash LaRue comic books and was a fan of Gene Autry and his horse Champion. On a Valentine's Day during his early youth, he received a card "from Mother and Dad" on which was pictured a white boy playing guitar. The white world was visible but only on the periphery. Cleve Sellers' paternal grandparents worked for whites. She cleaned clothes brought to the house; he was a gardener for a prominent white family.

Sellers joined Boy Scouts of America, the Central South Carolina Council, Troop No. 553, and in February 1960, the year that marked Scouting's golden anniversary, he attended the fifth National Jamboree in Colorado Springs, Colorado, as part of the Georgia-Alabama Council Division Jamboree Troop. His parents would pay $217.50 in two segments, and Sellers would leave Denmark on July 9 for Columbus, Georgia. The next day, a chartered, air-conditioned bus would transport participants to the Jamboree, returning them nearly a month later. For his efforts, Sellers received a Jamboree Adventure Reward.

He took his scouting seriously, attending retreats at the all-black Camp Brownlee and obtaining all the required merit badges. But before he could relish the accomplishment of achieving the Boy Scout's highest rank, his paperwork was misplaced. Then history thrust itself on the teenager, changing the course of his life. The failure to secure Eagle Scout status was an early disappointment. It wasn't until many years later, in 2007 when Sellers was 64, that Boy Scouts of America determined he could finally receive his Eagle designation. It was a moment that served as a kind of vindication, a reward made more meaningful, if bittersweet, because of the years of struggle that had intervened and the subsequent period of economic and social decay in black communities coping with the scourge of crack cocaine and mass incarceration, the new injustice of the so-called War on Drugs.

"I remember the challenges, and I remember the requirements to grow in rank and grow in knowledge and information," he told NPR reporter John Ydstie shortly after receiving his Eagle Scout designation. "[At] the National Jamboree...I had an opportunity there to meet a lot of other scouts from all around the world. The scouting program just provided a lot of alternatives to the kind of idleness that many young people today kind of experience....I am not comfortable with what I see that's happening with a lot of young people. And so one of the easiest things we can do is we can take a look at the Boy Scouts as one of the alternatives that we can utilize within the African-American community, and hopefully, we can get them into the rural communities and in the inner cities and a lot of other places."

Long before the pan-Africanism that many civil rights activists embraced during the 1970s and 1980s, before the achievements and disappointments of the tumultuous 1960s, there were days of innocence in Denmark. When Cleve Sellers was 10 or 11, he asked his father for a pony. The Sellers family was thrifty. Sellers Sr. was careful with the money he and his wife brought in, but they were able to live comfortably, without want and sometimes satisfy a whim or two.

"My father...tried to give us things that we needed as well as things that we wanted, because, first of all, they were older parents," Gwen Parker said. "Most parents didn't realize that, but they were older; much older." Gwen was born when her mother was 40. The parents were established in their careers and in their values by the time the children came along.

The elder Sellers went into the countryside one day and returned with a horse. It was a big horse that inspired fear, so he soon exchanged it for a Shetland pony which was kept in a small stable in the field beside the house. Cleve Sellers rode it, cared for it, attached its harnesses and hooked it to a cart. On one occasion, the horse was featured in a Voorhees homecoming parade.

Of course, no parent and no community, however insular, can protect a child from the world at large, and as Cleve Sellers rode his pony, read his comic books, admired his pastor, played with his friends and excelled at an institution that relied on old handed-down textbooks from white schools, the outside world came crashing in.

2

GENERATIONAL
DIVIDE

AN INDIVIDUAL'S IMPETUS for political action often is outrage and horror. Sellers was 10 years old when Emmett Till was
murdered in the Mississippi Delta. Though smaller and younger
than the 14-year-old boy from Chicago whose big physical stature
belied his age, Sellers saw himself mirrored in the mangled face
and broken body, photographs of which had circulated in the black
press and elsewhere. And he was shocked by the cruelty of Jim
Crow, by the sheer brutality human beings were capable of, and
which the political order made possible, even encouraged.

"I had a terrible time trying to react to that," Sellers said. "I
couldn't see a difference between the two of us....I took Jet

Magazine, with Till on the cover, to class. The teacher stopped and went through it and talked about it in class." Emmett Till did nothing wrong, she explained. He was guilty only of being a black kid in Mississippi. Till's murder left the young Sellers feeling uneasy. "There wasn't any use for us to get angry, there wasn't any use for us to [feel] defeated," he said. What was made apparent, what screamed at him in 1955, was that danger lurked everywhere in the South. Even a child was unsafe. "This is the challenge we faced."

The killing of Till is cited as one of the watershed events that triggered the direct-action phase of the civil rights movement of the 1950s and 1960s. It is said that Rosa Parks thought about Till while sitting on that bus in Montgomery, awaiting arrest. The crime shot fear into the hearts of Sellers' parents—and black parents everywhere, but especially in the South. As their sons and daughters soon began to join the movement, the older generation trembled at the thought of Till's corpse.

The teenager was murdered on Aug. 28, 1955, after an encounter with a white woman, 21-year-old Carolyn Bryant, at Bryant's Grocery and Meat Market in Tallahatchie County, Mississippi. Though the precise nature of the exchange remains unknown, Till was with friends and relatives in the store, and possibly was dared to say something to, or whistle at, the young wife of the store owner, Roy Bryant. He had grown up in a big northern city that, in the 1950s, saw some interaction between whites and blacks and was said to have possessed a photograph that included white Chicago friends. Times were changing up North, but not yet in the Deep South, as Till was soon to realize. His interracial encounter with Carolyn Bryant in the grocery store, with its innuendo (interpreted or invented), alluded to an absolute taboo of the time—sex between a black man and white woman. It was "one crime that warrants lynching," said South Carolina's Benjamin "Pitchfork" Tillman in an 1892 gubernatorial re-election campaign, "and

Governor as I am, I would lead a mob to lynch the negro who ravishes a white woman."

Till's alleged taunt prompted a quick response. Carolyn Bryant, claiming to be offended by the self-assured young Till, quickly told others about the episode. Roy Bryant and his half-brother, J.W. Milam, sought out Till that night and, with others in tow, kidnapped the boy, pistol-whipped him, forced him to strip naked, shot him in the head then dumped the body in the Tallahatchie River. Three days later, the bloated corpse was discovered eight miles downstream by two boys fishing. An investigation ensued, resulting in the acquittal of the defendants by an all-white jury. But a year later, protected by double jeopardy, Milam confessed to the murder in an interview with *Look* magazine.

> Well, what else could we do? He was hopeless. I'm no bully; I never hurt a nigger in my life. I like niggers—in their place—I know how to work 'em. But I just decided it was time a few people got put on notice. As long as I live and can do anything about it, niggers are gonna stay in their place. Niggers ain't gonna vote where I live. If they did, they'd control the government. They ain't gonna go to school with my kids. And when a nigger gets close to mentioning sex with a white woman, he's tired o' livin'. I'm likely to kill him. Me and my folks fought for this country, and we got some rights. I stood there in that shed and listened to that nigger throw that poison at me, and I just made up my mind. "Chicago boy," I said, "I'm tired of 'em sending your kind down here to stir up trouble. Goddam you, I'm going to make an example of you—just so everybody can know how me and my folks stand."

Less than four years after the lynching, on April 24, 1959, another set of interracial sex allegations and a second brutal murder would jolt America and send shock waves through a 14-year-old Sellers. Accused of kidnapping and raping a pregnant white woman in Pearl River County, Mississippi, Mack Charles Parker, 23, was jailed on unreliable circumstantial evidence, then, three days before his trial, attacked by white vigilantes who beat him bloody, drove him to the Louisiana state line, shot him in the chest at close range, tied chains to his body and dumped it into the Pearl River. The FBI immediately swooped in, interviewed hundreds of suspects and witnesses and put together a compelling case against the perpetrators. Among those under scrutiny was J.P. Walker, a former Pearl River County sheriff's deputy, who would be elected sheriff in 1963. The grand jury in the case indicted no one.

The killings of Emmett Till and Mack Charles Parker contributed significantly to Seller's political awakening; it thrust the harsh reality of the world upon him, a comfortable kid growing up middle class in Denmark, South Carolina, and it instilled in him a desire to do something that might make such murders, and the impunity with which they were committed, impossible.

"I'm inquisitive, I might have said something, too," Sellers mused regarding Till's alleged interaction with the white woman. "It was almost like that could have been me." And Parker's killing only drove home the point. How was it possible for a teenager increasingly made aware of injustice, accustomed to discussing current events at the dinner table and impressed by his activist priest to sit idly by?

Indeed, the outrage expressed by blacks in the wake of Till's murder was fueled in part by what was perceived as an assault on middle-class values, which necessarily were meant to extend to all people, regardless of race, who staked a claim on the American Dream. It was precisely this tension embodied in blacks who strove to become middle class—or who had already achieved mainstream success while simultaneously struggling under oppressive racist policies and social practices—that helped to ignite organized resistance and calls for equal opportunity and, later, integration.

IF EMMETT TILL'S MURDER was an initial rude awakening for the 10-year-old Sellers, then the event that catapulted him into adulthood was the start of the student movement in 1960. When Sellers learned about the Greensboro sit-ins, an effort by black students to demand service at a Woolworth lunch counter thereby challenging discriminatory laws, he absorbed an important message, one that thousands of other young people heard echoing across the country: If change was going to come, it would require student leadership, it would demand the fresh perspective and determined energy of the new generation, people at once idealistic and fed up. The injustice had gone on long enough. Timid parents and cautious grandparents no longer would have the same moral authority they enjoyed in the past. The stories of the elders who suffered under slavery and Jim Crow would not dissuade young people from taking risks; the stories would enrage them, compel them to look forward and force change.

Sellers, a high school student, susceptible like many others to this new psychology, heard about what was happening in Greensboro and decided to help organize a sit-in at Talbert's Drug Store lunch counter in Denmark. He had already become a young civil rights activist, leading the youth group of the NAACP in Denmark and planning with others a few minor protests. His father was uncomfortable with this activism. The elder Sellers was not one to deliberately rock a boat. Though whites and blacks didn't interact much, some of the town's white civic leaders, shop owners and farmers were members of the Ku Klux Klan, minding their business by day, then joining together after dark to affirm their superiority. Sellers

Sr. knew who they were, and he feared that his wife Pauline, who by that point worked as a teacher and nutritionist at the Denmark Area Trade Center, could lose her job if the family were branded as troublemakers because of their teenager, Cleve.

This concern over his son's civil rights activities was a source of protracted anxiety for both men. The elder Sellers, a stalwart and proud husband and father, was of a different generation, the one that mostly avoided direct confrontation with the dominant white power structure while fostering a sense of independence, economic self-sufficiency and educational success within the black community. Intellectually, he understood the imperative that drove his son, but he remained deeply worried for the well-being of the young Sellers. It was a tension that occasionally caused flare-ups at home and, early on, prompted a breach in their relationship and bouts of silence. But Sellers Sr. was not out of touch; he understood the changing times and acknowledged in his concerned and ambivalent way the need for direct action. Perhaps he was, over the years, simply finding ways to reconcile his experiences and worldview with those of his son, who was born at a particular moment in the history of the United States and who chose a selfless path.

But the beginning was tumultuous. When in early February 1960 the young Sellers heard about the Greensboro sit-ins, he sprang into action, joining junior college students in planning sessions for a comparable sit-in at the small Denmark drugstore's lunch counter that March. It was one of many such imitative events organized throughout the segregated South, though none captured as much national attention as the original, which stretched from days to weeks and showed young people opposed to the discriminatory status quo that they had power to affect change. In Denmark, about 14 young black men—all male junior college students (young women and high schoolers such as Sellers were excluded)—walked single-file to the drugstore, as local residents watched, full of anticipation and concern. "It was quiet, with a lot of people peeking out their windows," Sellers recalled. The students took turns at the soda fountain only to be refused service and arrested. Father Henry Grant, who had been involved in the planning, got them released from jail. The mobilization was at once thrilling and anticlimactic. The arrests riled the town's black community and motivated residents to push on with other anti-segregation initiatives, but the sit-in protest ended with a thud when, on the second attempt to occupy the drugstore, the students found it had been closed for the day. The owner had caught wind of the demonstration and pre-empted any additional drama.

ENERGIZED YOUNG PEOPLE, however, were not to be so easily quelled; they turned their attention to Voorhees itself, demanding change. The insurrection might have been avoided had Voorhees President John Potts thrown his support behind the rebel students. Instead, he chastised them to put an end to their demonstrations in town. They were making a difficult situation worse, he told them.

In fact, Potts was caught between students whose cause was obviously just (even if their tactics raised concern) and a powerful board of directors whose financial contributions kept the school afloat and whose influence in the community was significant. Indeed, it is worth remembering that black schools, like black funeral homes, law firms and prominent merchants, were part of a tightly woven fabric that protected African Americans during the Jim Crow years. For all of its injustice and inherent poverty, segregation forced blacks to rely on their own institutions and enterprises, and such efforts tended to engender a deep sense of purpose and commitment to community. Circumstances during these long years of oppression demanded solidarity and mutual protection among African Americans. An irony of the post-civil rights period is that this common cause was eroded by large social and economic currents that pushed some blacks into the consumer classes while marginalizing many others.

Potts' dilemma—he was caught between an unstoppable social force and a reticent group of overseers—was of no concern to young people determined to move their cause forward. At Voorhees, students demanded better food, later curfews, an end to compulsory class and chapel attendance and the right to demonstrate against racial discrimination. The school resisted, and the students redoubled their efforts in the fall. In October, the alumni association intervened, arranging a settlement: the school would concede to most of the demands if the students would end campus protests. Sellers, about to turn 16 on Nov. 8, was viewed as an unofficial leader of this student effort. "Students on the campus looked to me for direction," he wrote in his book, *The River of No Return*. "I don't know exactly why; it was probably a combination of things. I was well known, popular, a member of the basketball team, an honor student and zealously committed to the movement."

These were the first battle cries of the town's frustrated youth, who continued their political debates and strategic maneuvering on campus over the course of the school year, submitting a list of demands to President Potts. "We wanted better food in the cafeteria, an end to compulsory dress regulations and the right to demonstrate against off-campus racial discrimination when we saw fit," Sellers wrote.

Sellers set to work redirecting efforts from the campus to downtown Denmark. His plotting was interrupted in early March 1961 by a short visit to Rock Hill, South Carolina, where he met with civil rights activists involved in the Friendship Nine case, another episode of lunch counter sit-ins that produced the slogan "Jail No Bail." He drove there in Father Grant's Buick. Among the activists he got to know were Chuck McDew, Diane Bevel and Ruby Doris Smith, members of the recently formed Student Nonviolent Coordinating

Committee (SNCC). "We saw them in action," Sellers said, recalling that transformative moment in his life. Smith was a sophomore at Spelman College in Atlanta when the Freedom Rides began, and no stranger to activism. "I was tremendously impressed with her descriptions of the work that SNCC was doing with college students across the South," Sellers wrote in his memoir. That work, during the first few years of SNCC's 10-year run, consisted of large rallies and marches, efforts to desegregate public accommodations and voter registration drives in hard-to-reach rural counties.

SNCC HAD BEEN FORMED in February 1960 on the campus of Shaw University in Raleigh, North Carolina, pulled together by the indomitable civil rights matriarch Ella Baker who wanted students engaged in the sit-ins (now spreading far beyond Greensboro) to coordinate more closely and move from improvisation toward strategic protest. Among those attending the Shaw conference were Julian Bond from Atlanta, Charles McDew from South Carolina State College, Stokely Carmichael from Howard University and a group of activists from the Nashville Student Movement, including Diane Nash, John Lewis, James Bevel and Marion Barry, who would become SNCC's first chairman. Before long, Bob Moses would join the organization and lead a Mississippi voter registration drive that would transform SNCC from a strategy-devising group of activist-thinkers bent on coordinating various civil rights efforts into a stand-alone, project-oriented initiative focused on enfranchisement among the South's rural poor.

Julian Bond, the group's communications director during the first half of the 1960s, described the effort, and the group's broad accomplishments, in an essay published in 2000:

SNCC was founded in 1960 by southern student protesters

engaged in sit-in demonstrations against lunch-counter segregation. Within a year, it evolved from a coordinating agency to a hands-on organization, helping local leadership in rural and small-town communities across the South participate in a variety of protests, as well as in political and economic organizing campaigns. This set SNCC apart from the civil rights mainstream of the 1960s. Its members, its youth, and its organizational independence enabled SNCC to remain close to grassroots currents that rapidly escalated the southern movement from sit-ins to Freedom Rides, and then from voter drives to political organizing.

By 1965, SNCC fielded the largest staff of any civil rights organization in the South. It had organized nonviolent direct action against segregated facilities, as well as voter-registration projects, in Alabama, Arkansas, Maryland, Missouri, Louisiana, Virginia, Kentucky, Tennessee, Illinois, North and South Carolina, Georgia, and Mississippi; built two independent political parties and organized labor unions and agricultural cooperatives; and given the movement for women's liberation new energy. It inspired and trained the activists who began the "New Left." It helped expand the limits of political debate within black America, and broadened the focus of the civil rights movement. Unlike mainstream civil rights groups, which merely sought integration of blacks into the existing order, SNCC sought structural changes in American society itself.

Hearing that students amassed to organize for change inspired Sellers, though SNCC still was in his future. Of immediate concern was Denmark, and the key to desegregation efforts, he determined, was coordination. He contacted NAACP officials, who were reluctant to throw their support behind confrontational tactics and who admonished Sellers to "be patient." So in the spring of 1961 he went over their heads and, with backing from Father Grant, he secured a youth chapter charter from the NAACP's national office. Sellers, 16, became its leader, a move that formalized his civil rights activism.

His mother deferred to her son's judgment, even if townspeople were exerting some pressure on the family, intimating that she could lose her job at the trade school. And others told him to take it easy, push too hard. Voorhees officials voiced disapproval at Sellers' activism, but Father Grant's support did not waver. Cleveland Sellers Sr., in the meantime, was increasingly worried and critical, afraid that his son had stepped over the line and put the family at risk. The teenager would not be stopped. He decided to organize a rally at Rome Baptist Church (where Sellers Sr. was a member). He spent a month orchestrating the protest, garnering support from Columbia's civil rights activists, including the NAACP's South Carolina field secretary, the Reverend Isaiah DeQuincey Newman, inviting out-of-town speakers and coordinating with local civic leaders. A lawyer from the Atlanta office of the NAACP, Julie Wright, would give the keynote address. Flyers were distributed; signs went up all over town. Sellers wrote his speech, nervous about addressing a crowd publicly for the first time in his life.

Newman, a prominent figure active in the NAACP for three decades, preferred negotiation over direct action and was well-suited for the organization's brand of resistance and protest through legal challenges and community engagement. But the 49-year-old civil rights leader was nevertheless facing a stubborn form of institutional discrimination made all the more intractable because of the whiff of atrophy. Such discrimination increasingly called for the shunting aside of the non-confrontational approach.

Already, as a junior in high school, Sellers began to exemplify this new approach, one that would dominate the culminating phase of the civil rights movement. But in 1961, in rural Denmark, South Carolina, old fears still took hold, preventing Sellers from witnessing the fruits of his labor. The morning of the rally, his father insisted he quit his efforts and remain at home. "You cannot go," his father told him. "Your mother might lose her job. You just cannot go. I've been working all my life to build something for you. This demonstration and rallying is no good. If you keep on, you're going to destroy everything. Let some of the others do it. You've done your part."

This denial, though caused by a father's legitimate worry for the safety of his son and the security of his family, would drive a wedge in their relationship. Soon, a father's conservatism, conditioned by a life subjected to Jim Crow and its peculiar hazards, would run head-on into the son's radicalism. The rally went on without Sellers, but the wind was not in Denmark's sails. The youth chapter of the NAACP petered out. Black residents failed to follow up with action. Voorhees officials, perturbed by Father Grant's civil rights activism, arranged to have him removed from St. Philip's Chapel. Sellers, thinking about college, thinking about his father's admonitions and fear, thinking about the loss of a role model and the hard work yet to be done, was ready to leave. He wanted to attend a black college in the South, even if his grades might have gained him access to a reputable northern institution. He chose Howard University.

It would disappoint him and, in so doing, drive him to SNCC.

3 ENTER THE STUDENTS

THE YOUNG SELLERS was a product of parents who prepared their children to excel and, consequently, strove to set the stage through hard work and high expectations. And he was, among other things, an intellectual, encouraged to think through his circumstances and evaluate the conditions that produced segregation in the South and, more broadly, racial inequality worldwide. Already in 1960, the 16-year-old was asserting his identity as a member of the African diaspora who happened to grow up in Denmark. Already he had an inkling that the movement's effort to integrate public accommodations and register blacks to vote was an inadequate goal, though perhaps he was still too young to know precisely why. When he arrived at Howard University in 1962, driven away from South Carolina in part by his father's impositions and in part by his nascent political awakening, he found he was a black sheep in a herd of buttoned-up achievers. At Howard, where middle-class values were taught and rebellion discouraged, he discovered the student-run Nonviolent Action Group, an arm of the Student Nonviolent Coordinating Committee, which campaigned for civil rights in the area. Sellers decided to join. It was not possible for him to remain on the sidelines in the fight for justice.

Founded in Washington, D.C., in 1867 by a group of Congregationalists, Howard began as a modest seminary to educate black clergy and soon added schools for the study of liberal arts and medicine. By the early 1960s, it was receiving a federal appropriation of $7 million, employing about 700 faculty and enrolling about 7,000 students. Its campus was nicknamed "The Mecca" because of the school's appeal to ambitious, often middle-class black students.

Even before his admission to Howard, Sellers' political sympathies and fashion inclinations, such as they were, leaned hard in a black populist direction. He might have grown up middle class, but he was no bourgeois. His burgeoning sense of cultural identity, which would flower during the Black Power period of SNCC's later years and reach an apex as pan-Africanism informed a new-found collective purpose with international reach, was already manifested in the teenage activist. He grew his hair long; he dressed informally. He kept his sights on the movement and its participants. At Howard, "you were an outcast if you wore jeans," Sellers said. Yet he favored them over the pressed shirts and thin ties most young men wore. The young women, instead, donned dresses, stockings and high-heeled shoes. The 1951 MGM movie *Quo Vadis* starred Robert Taylor wearing his hair short, a little curly on top, close-cropped on the sides, and this became a standard signifier of the black middle class. Almost all the male students at Howard wore their hair short. Not Sellers. It wasn't an Afro yet, but it didn't have that sculpted look of the *Quo Vadis* haircut. "So that was one of the things that many of the other students rejected"—it wasn't appropriate Howard University style. "They would make you kind of a social outcast. But that was OK."

He had expected to find many other young people sympathetic to the movement and ready to mobilize. "I was thinking Howard would be the hotbed [where] students had 'activism' written all over their faces," he said. Instead he discovered that a majority of students were focused on other goals; they were ambivalent about what was happening in the Deep South. He had come to Howard with an ostensible interest in mechanical engineering and a lingering taste in his mouth of direct action only to find himself marginalized by prevailing attitudes which favored personal achievement over collective justice. "You did not want to look like a poor or an ordinary black person at Howard," Sellers said. "You wanted to look like you were ambitious." Sellers didn't look ambitious, at least not as if his primary goal was to climb a corporate ladder or otherwise ingratiate himself among members of the country's power structure. "No, I thought I was representing some of the best of what blacks had to offer in terms of who I was, in reflecting, or trying to reflect, who I was and where I'd come from," he said. But in the eyes of his fellow college students, he looked like a rebel, and they kept their distance. "I didn't like how they treated me or how they relegated me [to the margins] because of what I wore and how I dressed. I had a tough time with that one."

IT TOOK A FEW MONTHS, but eventually Sellers ran across a few students with their ears to the pavement, politically engaged people who referred him to other politically engaged people, "and I began to associate with some of those people." One of those people included a brilliant, exuberant young man with Caribbean roots, Stokely Carmichael, then a sophomore. Sellers began attending meetings of the Nonviolent Action Group (NAG), whose mission was to confront racism with nonviolent direct action. Carmichael, born in Trinidad and raised in New York City where he attended the Bronx High School of Science, viewed Howard University as a gateway and a nurturing environment where learning and activism went hand in hand.

"Howard University would open up vast new horizons for me," Carmichael wrote in his autobiography. "No doubt about that. Without question, I received a unique education there. And no question, it was qualitatively and substantively different from any education I could possibly have had at Harvard or anywhere else in the world." The contradictions were not lost on him, however. He understood that Howard was an institution dependent on government funding and, therefore, in no position to buck the system. Its administrators walked a fine line, educating the new generation of African Americans to improve the world (among the lawyers who had worked on the *Brown* case were Howard graduates), but discouraging "any activity on the part of the students that was likely to offend 'powerful white folk.'"

"As you might well imagine, we in NAG took a slightly different position," Carmichael wrote. "Inasmuch as this nation had enslaved Africans and continued to discriminate against them, thereby crippling them educationally, we felt that the least the nation owed the African community was excellent resources by which to educate ourselves. Educationally, we felt America owed us many more than one federally supported school. As a matter of historical obligation, not charity."

Carmichael was not concerned about propriety. He was unin-
terested in being polite, rejecting paternalism outright. "We felt,
especially as we grew more confident in our organizing skills, that
we students could organize effective pressure inside the nation's
capital, on international forums, and before the world media, to
ensure that the U.S. government met its obligations to black education. We understood that the Howard administration would
need to stay aloof—publicly—but at least they should not hinder
us. The world was changing, wasn't it?"

SELLERS WAS GLAD to have discovered NAG, relieved to be
among kindred spirits. That first meeting he attended was a
small turning point, one of many that would define Sellers' path.
"That's when I met all these interesting people," he said, "and
[Carmichael] was just one of them. He was one of these scholars....He was always kind of upbeat, kind of joking around. It
was just [brief] moments when he was serious about anything we
were talking about." And then he would be short and to the point,
Sellers said. "The more I knew him, the more I realized that was
part of his persona....He talked all the time. I didn't mind it. I
wasn't a talker, I was always the quiet one."

Sellers, unhappy at Howard where he stubbornly refused to conform, was spending much of his time strategizing with Carmichael.
The two soon became close friends, determined to play a role in
the movement, eager to put into practice the ideas thrown about
on campus. As NAG activists, during the winter of 1962 they were
de facto members of SNCC, privy to the larger organization's plans
for tackling the problem of disenfranchisement in the rural South.
But there was work to be done in Washington, D.C. "Our primary
task was demonstrating," Sellers wrote in *The River of No Return*.

"Whenever black people in the city of Washington needed pickets, they would get in touch with NAG." The group of Howard activists, which included Courtland Cox, Murial Tillinghast, Stanley Wise, Bill Mahoney, Ed Brown and Phil Hutchins, would picket various businesses that had not yet fully desegregated, and also government offices and the White House. Already in late 1962 there was a pervasive sense among students that the federal government was failing in its duty to advance the cause of justice, protect demonstrators and quell endemic violence in the South. "By the end of my second semester at Howard, I went on campus only to eat, sleep, attend classes and participate in periodic NAG rallies," Sellers wrote. "I spent the rest of my time demonstrating and getting to know the people who lived in the huge black ghetto surrounding the campus."

NAG invited guest speakers, activists in the movement, to address students. The year before Sellers arrived, Howard had hosted a momentous debate between Bayard Rustin, a strong proponent of nonviolence and an organizer of the first Freedom Ride in 1947, and Nation of Islam activist Malcolm X. Rustin had spoken of the need for a coalition between black activists and organized labor, insisting that the path to social and economic enfranchisement was paved with jobs. He was looking ahead to the latter part of the decade when the movement would shift its attention from integration to larger issues of class and the insidious ways in which disenfranchisement can be perpetuated through economic policies. The students of NAG were impressed with Rustin's intelligence and persistence but most favored Malcolm's forceful argument for self-determination. The debate was part of a series NAG launched called Project Awareness. Rustin, who had provided instrumental support to both NAG and SNCC, argued that blacks should fight nonviolently for full access to America's social and economic systems; Malcolm argued that blacks should achieve autonomy from whites. His articulation of black nationalism mesmerized many in attendance, especially Carmichael and his NAG colleagues, who for the first time began to think seriously about a form of self-determination that was independent from the white power structure.

Those were the ideas already swirling about when Sellers arrived at Howard in the fall of 1962. In Washington, a storm was brewing, and at the end of his freshman year Sellers decided he would remain there. He was not keen on returning to his father's house in Denmark; that was seen as a retreat, and Sellers was not about to retreat from the movement now.

EARLY THE FOLLOWING YEAR, Sellers got to know Malcolm X better. The Muslim firebrand, who had been assigned by the Nation of Islam to Mosque No. 4 in Washington, D.C., visited the Howard campus again in the months before the 1963 March on Washington to continue the conversation about black identity and pride. "He wasn't hard to find. We used to find him all the time," Sellers said. After a campus appearance, Malcolm would retire with several others to Carmichael's apartment to continue the debate well into the early morning hours. This was five years before Carmichael would raise his fist and cry "Black Power," advancing a revised political agenda that, in many ways, had its roots in Malcolm's 1961 oratory.

Encounters with Malcolm always resulted in stimulating conversations. "He called us 'his students,'" Sellers recalled. They debated the idea of nonviolent resistance. They disagreed. They stimulated each other's minds. They refined their thinking. Malcolm, strongly nationalistic and Afro-centric in those days, would demand to know from other blacks where they were from. One man from Cleveland replied by stating the city of his birth, then the town in the South where his grandparents grew up.

Malcolm was dissatisfied by such answers, repeating the question with more emphasis on the word "from," as if that might trigger an important realization. He'd say, "If a cat has kittens in an oven, that doesn't make them biscuits," and hope his interlocutors would understand that an African transferred to a foreign land remains African at heart, no matter what happens to him, Sellers said. And he would employ a coffee metaphor to dissuade "his students" from diluting their blackness: First you pour strong black coffee into the cup, then you add cream and what do you get? Malcolm liked to debate the students. It sharpened his arguments, gave him food for thought, Sellers said. "He was trying to impress us, and he had found intellectual young people who would [appreciate]…that discussion," especially Carmichael, a philosophy major.

But most of the Howard students didn't give in. They argued that in the South, nonviolence was more effective. They explained the significance of the church as a central beacon for blacks. They described the experience of marching through small towns as glass bottles flew through the air and hate pulsated from curbsides like August heat, where the mountains of prejudice were so steep it took a determined, systematic effort to climb them. An arsenal of harsh words and threats was of little use to Southern blacks, they told their guest of honor. Malcolm listened. His biting retorts were ego-bruising, Sellers said.

The Howard activists occasionally would run into Malcolm when they were out and about. Bodyguards usually recognized Sellers and his cadre of fellow NAG and SNCC members, allowing them to approach.

In NAG with Sellers were Ivanhoe Donaldson, Charlie Cobb and H. Rap Brown, who would play pivotal roles in SNCC in the years to come. "Cleve and Rap especially would soldier on through some very, very dangerous times in the late sixties," Carmichael wrote. "Both would be shot, jailed, and survive intact and strong.

Rap and Cleve are two brothers who went the distance and then some more...and paid some heavy dues."

WHILE RACISM WAS pervasive throughout the country, and manifested itself in sometimes insufferable ways in northern cities, the epicenter of racial injustice was in the South, especially Mississippi and Alabama where African Americans were mostly poor subsistence farmers kept down by decades of Jim Crow. Blacks in the South had for generations endured intimidation campaigns, sometimes orchestrated by the political establishment, sometimes by vigilante groups. They were required to pay poll taxes and pass literacy exams, fooled into believing their vote couldn't make a difference. The so-called literacy test often came in the form of a registration application that asked a series of questions, including name, date, place of residence and employer. "The most trivial of errors—like the absence of a comma in the date or a discrepancy in punctuation—would often result in an immediate failure," Marsh wrote in *God's Long Summer*. Any black who dared to challenge segregation by registering to vote often found himself suddenly unemployed or worse—at risk of losing property or life to the Ku Klux Klan or other vigilantes. Voter registration clerks routinely furnished registration information, including addresses, to employers and members of the white Citizens' Councils, and local newspapers published the names of people who had filed an application.

But the new generation of educated, justice-minded students, black and white, essentially believed that the key to changing the system was to play by its rules and create a Southern bloc of black voters who would replace established segregationists and white supremacists with people who actually represented the population fairly. Racists knew this, too, and fought back hard, with evolving strategies implemented both in Washington, D.C., and in local communities.

White supremacy was the status quo in the South until World War II, when the federal government began to experiment with integrated military units. The South's white leaders recognized that change was forcing them to adapt, to modify their arguments and alter their tactics. The strategy of "supremacy" therefore became one of "segregation." Eventually "segregation" gave way to "equalization." But no matter the terminology or softened rhetoric, the goal was to keep the races separate; the prevailing worry was "mongrelization," and the preferred political tactic was to couch racist policies in a "states' rights" argument.

Until 1960 and the student-led sit-in movement, the dominant civil rights organization in the U.S. was the NAACP, which relied primarily on legal challenges to existing laws and social practices. It criticized injustice, often forcefully, but did not advocate overturning the political system. Rather, it functioned within it. Its approach was effective. It culminated in 1954 with the *Brown* decision. But it was also slow since it can take years for a legal case to make its way through the courts and result in a firm decision. Members of the Congress of Racial Equality (CORE) and SNCC, as well as other young activists, often chided the NAACP for its systematic methodology and insider status, preferring a more confrontational approach that could set injustice in relief and force change more quickly.

There were exceptions to this general attitude among the movement's young generation—NAACP leaders, such as Medgar Evers, who willingly assumed frontline positions in the escalating fight against segregation and discrimination, were welknown and much admired. Evers was NAACP field secretary in Jackson, Mississippi, at the time of his 1963 murder and had a long list of accomplishments involving direct action. He assisted with an organized boycott of white businesses and was instrumental in desegregating the University of Mississippi thanks to his mentorship of James Meredith. Other NAACP leaders who would join the constellation of important civil rights activists included Rosa Parks, Walter White, Roy Wilkins and Septima Clark. Clark, a school teacher in the South Carolina Lowcountry, was fired from her job because of her NAACP membership. She went on to become a central figure in the voter rights campaign, teaching literacy in the Citizenship Schools and becoming an active participant in planning sessions held at Highlander Folk School in Tennessee.

Little of this was lost on a young Cleve Sellers who became acquainted with this history growing up at home, who flirted briefly with the NAACP as a youth leader and who debated the merits and pitfalls of enfranchisement versus self-sufficiency. "With segregation, we had to build a protective cocoon," he said. But then as African Americans mobilized to break down the superstructure of Jim Crow, new lessons were learned about what constituted victory and which tactics were most effective in achieving it.

The Southern Christian Leadership Conference's (SLCC) reliance on boycotts, marches and protests—tactics that, combined with the philosophy of nonviolence, garnered much media attention—was certainly an essential part of the movement, though it contrasted with the daily toil in the Deep South undertaken by SNCC activists, grueling and dangerous work that typically went unnoticed except by the local people fighting for or against change. Julian Bond neatly summed up the prevailing attitudes toward the NAACP and SCLC:

> The NAACP was outlawed in Alabama in 1956 and did not begin operating there again until 1964, although NAACP activists continued under other sponsorship. In 1962, the NAACP had one field secretary each in South Carolina, Florida, Alabama, and Mississippi, and a regional staff headquartered in Atlanta.

The Southern Christian Leadership Conference (SCLC) hired its first field secretary in 1960; in 1964, SCLC staff numbered sixty-two. By summer 1965, SCLC had staff in every southern state except Florida and Tennessee. Much of the organization's work, like the NAACP's effort, was conducted through affiliates. The historian Adam Fairclough wrote, "SCLC has to adopt a strategy of 'hit and run' striking one target at a time." SCLC's willingness to run as well as hit provoked consistent criticism from SNCC, which organized the same communities for years rather than months or weeks.

"SCLC mobilized," someone said. "SNCC organized."

Just two years after its formation, SNCC had 11 staff members in southwest Georgia, and 20 staff members throughout Mississippi, Bond wrote. By August 1963, SNCC had ramped up its Mississippi operations even more and solidified its presence in a dozen communities, as well as in Selma, Alabama; Danville, Virginia; and Pine Bluff, Arkansas. The Atlanta headquarters was Ground Zero for 12 workers, 60 field secretaries and 121 full-time volunteers.

If the Montgomery Bus Boycott galvanized activists around the idea of direct action, thus inexorably shifting the emphasis of the movement, the organizational efforts of 1960 established the major components of that movement and set them in motion. SNCC brought together a critical mass of educated young people and admonished them to take matters into their own hands. After SNCC's initial gathering in Raleigh, follow-up meetings in Atlanta, in May and October, established the group's base, helped forge its mission and defined its tactical arsenal. Ella Baker, referring to the sit-ins, spoke of the importance of pursuing goals beyond integration per se. Using a metaphor that would resonate across the decade, she said that the effort was "much bigger than a hamburger or even a giant-sized Coke."

When Bob Moses arrived in Atlanta from his teaching position in New York, looking for a non-existent position with SCLC, he was quickly directed to Jane Stembridge, SNCC's only full-time staffer at the time, and put to work licking envelopes. Soon he was proposing to launch a rural voter registration drive which would have the double effect of aiding poor, disenfranchised blacks in the South and strengthening SNCC's focus and purpose, distinguishing it among the myriad of civil rights organizations functioning at the time. SNCC, now with Moses as its field secretary, was setting the stage and was therefore ready when the Chicago-based Congress of Racial Equality initiated the Freedom Rides in 1961. This effort to desegregate public accommodations drew many—blacks and whites, northerners and southerners—into the movement, and it was SNCC, now rooted in the South where most of the action was, that could best accommodate them.

IN JUNE 1963 Baynard Rustin contacted NAG: he needed help organizing a big gathering for jobs and justice. The March on Washington for Jobs and Freedom, a central event of 1963 that drew about 250,000 and featured memorable speeches by participants (including Martin Luther King's "Dream" speech), was originally conceived as a disruption meant to draw attention to acute problems: institutional racism and economic strain. It was designed as a form of confrontation and challenge, a wake-up call to the indifferent masses, a reminder that segregation was not a problem only for blacks. "The march was being made 'respectable,'" wrote Sellers, who assisted organizers by making thousands of cheese sandwiches and creating thousands of placards for participants to carry. This was not likely the result of any single strategic decision but, rather, a consequence of success. As word of the march spread, more people, including members of labor unions and church institutions, white liberals and others, wanted to be part of it. The Justice Department endorsed the event. And as more people joined the effort, they were admonished to "keep the rhetoric within bounds." Had it been co-opted, as some said? Watered down? Compromised? John Lewis, then chairman of SNCC, was one of many slated to give a speech from the steps of the Lincoln Memorial, and he intended to challenge the federal government, apply the concept of slavery to current conditions, threaten to "take matters into our own hands" and allude to a symbolic second civil war, this one led by freedom fighters marching "through the South, through the heart of Dixie, the way Sherman did." It was a war that could not avoid violence. "We will pursue our own 'scorched earth' policy," Lewis wrote in the original version of his speech.

But union and religious leaders objected to the fiery rhetoric and demanded that Lewis tone it down. In a caucus hastily thrown together that included King, James Forman and march organizer A. Philip Randolph, the young Freedom Rider, who two years before was beaten in Rock Hill, South Carolina, as he exited a bus destined for the deepest reaches of the Deep South, relented, making extensive changes to the speech. Cut from Lewis' remarks:

> It seems to me that the Albany [Georgia] indictment [of civil rights activists] is part of a conspiracy on the part of the federal government and local politicians in the interest of expediency. I want to know, which side is the federal government on? The revolution is at hand, and we must free ourselves of the chains of political and economic slavery. The nonviolent revolution is saying, "We will not wait for the courts to act, for we have been waiting for hundreds of years. We will not wait for the President, the Justice Department, nor Congress, but we will take matters into our own hands and create a source of power, outside of any

national structure, that could and would assure us a victory.... "

We cannot depend on any political party, for both the Democrats and the Republicans have betrayed the basic principles of the Declaration of Independence. We all recognize the fact that if any radical social, political and economic changes are to take place in our society, the people, the masses, must bring them about....

The revolution is a serious one. Mr. Kennedy is trying to take the revolution out of the streets and put it into the courts. Listen, Mr. Kennedy. Listen, Mr. Congressman. Listen, fellow citizens. The black masses are on the march for jobs and freedom, and we must say to the politicians that there won't be a "cooling-off" period.

All of us must get in the revolution....

At this stage of his life, Sellers was little more than a spectator among hundreds of thousands, a low-level operative focused on practical matters: corresponding with allies and supplying sustenance and signage. "With the March on Washington, I called the SNCC people and said, 'We want your energy and we want you here,'" he recalled. "And so we got Joyce Ladner and some of the Mississippi folk, and then the Howard NAG group, and we all had different assignments, running errands, making signs, making sandwiches. We did it all." He was skeptical of the competing agendas and rhetorical bombast, disappointed in the censorship of Lewis' speech and SNCC's willingness to go along with the changes. Sellers was impressed by the large turnout and glad that organizers lobbied for fair labor practices, raising the minimum wage, banning discrimination in public housing, desegregating schools and more. But he couldn't forget Malcolm X's earlier critique of the march, in which the Muslim radical, leery of any expressed hope for cooperation and compromise between the oppressed and the oppressors occupying the neo-Classical buildings nearby, referred to the event as the "Farce on Washington."

"For me, the march was anticlimactic," Sellers wrote. "I had seen too much.... I spent most of the long afternoon wandering aimlessly through the huge throng of 250,000 people: watching, listening and thinking."

4 INITIATION BY FIRE

LESS THAN TWO HOURS from Howard University, in the small Maryland town of Cambridge, black residents were fighting segregation in 1962-63 and encountering much resistance from the white community. On campus, Cleveland Sellers and his NAG colleagues attended classes and debated the issues while, across the Chesapeake Bay, African Americans confronted persistent discrimination, police brutality and high unemployment. Cambridge was devolving into one of the flashpoints of the civil rights struggle, and it would soon envelop Sellers and his fellow freedom fighters. By the spring of 1964, Sellers would find himself at the epicenter of a violent confrontation in Cambridge—an initiation by fire—that in some ways foreshadowed a future conflagration, one that four years later would reshape his entire life.

In a city that was one-third black, Gloria Richardson, a leader and founder of the SNCC-affiliated Cambridge Nonviolent Action Committee (CNAC), joined other residents in organizing protests and boycotts of white merchants downtown and called not just for the end of discrimination but for genuine social and economic equality. By March 1963, segregation was still enforced by a number of merchants and city officials, but blacks were beginning to focus on more than public accommodations. Housing conditions, economic injustice and other concerns increasingly were galvanizing the local protest movement, and Richardson, then in her 40s, took the lead, organizing a series of demonstrations against white power and attempting to negotiate solutions that would create lasting change. It was the student-led nonviolent part of the movement that captured her imagination and propelled her to action. "I could never work with the NAACP. It took them too long to make decisions," she said. "There was something direct, something real about the way the kids waged nonviolent war. This was the first time I saw a vehicle I could work with." The situation in Cambridge was deteriorating; demonstrations were ineffective, and black residents enduring the double-humiliation of segregation and chronic unemployment of nearly 30 percent were growing restless. The demonstrations accumulated in size and frequency. The threat of violence loomed.

In June 1963 the threat gave way to the real thing. Maryland state troopers were called in, but sided with whites. White mobs attacked blacks. Blacks armed themselves, formed a perimeter around demonstrators and prepared to shoot back if provoked. Nonviolence was a tactic put to use by protestors, but only to a point: blacks would not turn the other cheek when bullets were flying. On the night of June 14, someone set alight a few white-owned businesses located in the Second Ward, the black part of town. Shots were exchanged. Martial law was declared after CNAC refused to agree to a one-year moratorium on protests. The National Guard was called in. Tension increased. On July 12, whites attacked a group of blacks sitting in a restaurant, provoking a street brawl. Later that night, the violence escalated into riot, with shots fired again between whites and blacks, and more white-owned shops set ablaze. The National Guard reasserted its presence, remaining in the city through July 7, 1964.

The segregationists were stubborn in Cambridge. When U.S. Assistant Attorney General Burke Marshall, then in charge of the Civil Rights Division, and Attorney General Robert Kennedy intervened, calling Richardson, John Lewis of SNCC and other activists to Washington on July 23 to negotiate the "Treaty of Cambridge," the wary black representatives agreed to a five-point deal, which included the desegregation of public accommodations and schools, new public housing, job appointments for blacks and the formation of a Human Relations Commission in exchange for an end to the demonstrations. But local hardline white segregationists would have none of it. They petitioned the Dorchester Business & Citizens Association which arranged a referendum vote to scuttle the agreement. Almost certainly the referendum would have failed; blacks and moderate whites outnumbered the hardliners. But Richardson called on blacks to boycott the vote, claiming that liberty and justice are not determined by the ballot box. "A first-class citizen does not beg for freedom," she said at the time. "A first-class citizen does not plead to the white power structure to give him something that the whites have no power to give or take away. Human rights are human rights, not white rights."

By the start of the 1963-64 school year, the situation in Cambridge was stalemated. "Gloria was holding the movement together with the help of SNCC staff, and students from NAG and other schools came in regularly to help with workshops, registration, and petition drives or to march in demonstrations, but with no victories and little progress to report, local people were getting tired and discouraged," wrote Stokely Carmichael in his autobiography. Discouragement turned to rage in Cambridge in the spring of 1964 when the presidential primary campaign began. Alabama Governor George Wallace, the staunch segregationist and face of Southern resistance, declared his candidacy and decided to kick off his Maryland campaign in the hotbed of racial unrest: Cambridge. He would address a whites-only audience at the local skating rink. Richardson called her SNCC and NAG contacts to ask for reinforcements. She wanted a strong turnout of protestors at Wallace's event. Sellers, Carmichael, Courtland Cox, Michael Thelwell and a few others responded immediately, descending upon the intransigent town to join the reinvigorated protests. The activists called a meeting and decided to march that night to the skating rink, hundreds strong. On Race Street they encountered a blockade. "Ranks of guardsmen in full battle dress, carrying carbines with fixed bayonets and standing in close order, completely block the road," Carmichael wrote.

> A few carried enormous airfield searchlights. Behind them you can see and hear a large crowd of whites. Silently we march up within fifteen yards. Gloria moves up and engages the general [George W. Gelston]. It is so quiet we can hear every word. He orders her to disperse the march. You have no permit, he says. Does George Wallace need a permit? she asks.
>
> She stands for a moment. A slender woman looking at a solid wall of soldiers towering over her. Then she pushes the rifle aside, tries to step through the ranks, and is immediately arrested.... When the general bellows at us to disperse, we all sit down.

The troops begin to put on gas masks. We have expected that and carry damp cloths to protect our faces against tear gas. The standard drill is to get low, cover your face, breathe through the damp cloths, and wait for the gas to disperse. We are ready. No big thing.

When authorities arrested Richardson and two fellow protestors, an enraged Sellers stepped forward, provoking a national guardsman to swing the butt of his rifle at his head. Sellers ducked and grabbed the gun, "wrestling over the rifle while everyone else watched," he recounted in his memoir. Soon he pushed away, looking for an escape route as Gelston shouted "Arrest that man!"— but too many people crowded the area, so Sellers fell in with the surge of accumulating bodies attempting to protect him from the guardsmen. The authorities struggled to reach for Sellers but were bitten or kicked back by others in the swarm. The vicious tussle between protestors and guardsmen failed to extricate Sellers, causing Gelston to call back his men and order the next move. As Guardsmen donned gas masks, the protestors prepared themselves. "While we were busily tying our dampened handkerchiefs to our faces, a guardsman dressed in a strange uniform headed toward us. He looked like an astronaut. His uniform was iridescent and gave off a soft, eerie glow. He was wearing a helmet. And there were a couple of big tanks strapped to his back. There was a tube leading from the tanks and he was holding the end of it, a long funnel, in his right hand.... The strange contraption was not a gas gun. It was a converted flame thrower. The tanks on the guardsman's back did not contain tear gas, either. They were filled with some kind of nauseating gas. By the time we realized all this, it was too late," Sellers wrote.

Next, mayhem. Carmichael got a blast directly in his face and blacked out. Protestors, at least those still capable of fleeing, staggered away with guardsmen advancing in large units, their boots slamming upon the pavement, their weapons rattling. "I am certain that a lot of people would have been seriously injured if a small group of black men had not started shooting at the guardsmen in order to slow them down," Sellers wrote. Eventually, he made it to the CNAC office where he encountered a desperate Carmichael, gasping for breath. Sellers and a few others dragged Carmichael to a car and rushed off, first to a police station where they met hostile officers who denied there was any problem, then to the fire station where they were told an ambulance could take Carmichael to the hospital. Instead, a group of troopers at the fire station attempted to detain the injured protesters, prompting one, SNCC photographer Cliff Vaughn, to resist. "One of the guardsmen rammed a bayonet through his leg," Sellers wrote. "Blood spurted everywhere."

After that, they did what they were told, clamoring into a truck where, to their surprise, they met Richardson and the two men who were arrested earlier. Carmichael was taken to the hospital. The next morning, recovered, he walked out and returned to the CNAC office where Brigadier General Gelston was holding forth about outside agitators and Communists. "'You,' he cried. 'What are you doing here? You're supposed to be under arrest,'" Carmichael recounted in his autobiography. "'What are you doing here?' I ask. 'You're a war criminal. Chemical warfare against unarmed folks. You should be in jail, not me. Unless you have a warrant, *you* better leave.'" He did. And so did Carmichael, before troopers could return. Sellers, Richardson and the others were jailed for two days at the Pikesville Armory, then returned to Cambridge, where they spent a couple hours in the city jail before getting bailed out by CNAC.

This would end Sellers' first life-threatening misadventure of the 1960s. He had run the gauntlet; he had been jailed for the first time; he had been fully initiated into the movement. He had the scars to prove it. He and Carmichael were called back to Washington, D.C., where they would recruit volunteers for one of the most important initiatives of the struggle, the Mississippi Summer Project, a massive grassroots voter registration drive and watershed moment in the history of the nation, for it would help galvanize the broader public around the civil rights cause, lead to the formation of a new, black-led political party that would challenge the status quo and plant the seeds of black nationalism, which would burst through the soil in 1965 and 1966 and begin to flower.

But one could argue that the seeds of black nationalism and self-determination were sown also in Cambridge, Maryland, in 1963, soon after the March on Washington. Cambridge showed that the realization of King's dream would require more than character, patience and determination. It would require mobilization. It would require confrontation and enormous sacrifice. It would require empowerment—not bestowed by whites but self-actualized by blacks. "In some ways, Cambridge was unique," wrote historian Annette Brock. "It was the first grass-roots movement outside the deep South; it was one of the first campaigns to focus on economic conditions rather than just civil rights, the Kennedy administration intervened on a broader scale than ever before (the actual signing of an 'Accords' took place); nonviolence was questioned as a tactic; and it was the first major movement of which a woman was the leader."

Something else happened in Cambridge: a new kind of polarization that pitted "radicals" interested in much more than integration against an old guard willing to block their way no matter what. In other places, efforts of the freedom fighters garnered at least some sympathy among moderates, and even prompted liberal whites to join the movement. But in the fight for equality on Maryland's Eastern Shore, there seemed to be little room for moderates.

"The liberal or moderate center collapsed in Cambridge in 1963 and 1964," wrote Peter Levy in his *Civil War on Race Street*. "At the same time, this led many to describe Cambridge as unique or unusual and helps explain the marginalization of Cambridge by scholars. Yet looking backward with the advantage of historical hindsight, we can see that the developments in Cambridge presaged several broader trends." Those lessons certainly were not lost on Sellers and his "radical" colleagues.

As for Wallace, he enjoyed a remarkable showing at the ballot box, collecting 44.5 percent of the vote in Maryland's Democratic primary and barely losing to Sen. Daniel Brewster, President Lyndon Johnson's man. Wallace won 16 of the state's 23 counties, including the whole of the Eastern Shore.

5 A TURNING POINT

IF THE CIVIL RIGHTS MOVEMENT—really a cluster of often barely coordinated efforts waged in disparate places at the grassroots level—succeeded in changing the country, it was Freedom Summer of 1964 that irrevocably changed the civil rights movement. What happened in Mississippi in 1964, and at the Democratic National Convention in Atlantic City that August, altered the tactics, attitudes and social framework of the movement. It energized thousands of new activists even as it frustrated veterans; it led to direct political action with the formation of the Mississippi Freedom Democratic Party, then shattered whatever optimism remained among SNCC members about America's democratic system, tipping the balance between cooperation and confrontation. "Afterward, things could never be the same," Sellers wrote in his memoir. "Never again were we lulled into believing that our task was exposing injustices so that the 'good' people of America could eliminate them." For Sellers and many other civil rights activists, progress now would depend on self-preservation and black autonomy.

In the fall of 1963, SNCC had organized a mock election for governor in Mississippi to demonstrate the will to vote among African Americans. Many white people believed that African Americans didn't really want to engage in the political process. The so-called Mississippi Freedom Vote of 1963 was merely an exercise in democracy that neither saw anyone elected to public office nor inspired the Democratic Party machine to make accommodations for the disenfranchised, at least not immediately. But when 83,000 blacks turned out to vote at churches, barbershops and other community centers November 2-4, 1963, it did demonstrate to organizers the will of the people and the potential for a grassroots campaign whose main goal was political empowerment. Put simply by Sellers, who spent that fall at Howard University attending classes and organizing college students, the idea of the Freedom Vote "was to show that if blacks could vote, they would," and to get them acquainted with the process. At Howard, NAG students were tapped into the movement, keeping up to date on developments through a vast network of interconnected activists and thanks to newsletters, phone calls and official communications by civil rights groups. The grapevine was robust and well nourished.

Down south, SNCC leaders, joined by others from CORE and the Council of Federated Organizations (COFO), were canvassing Mississippi's Delta and signing up participants. SNCC's Atlanta office prepared flyers that included photographs meant to rile up black residents so they would vote in the mock election. One, a picture of a helmeted white guardsman, featured the caption, "Is he protecting you?" Another image—two young children sitting on a curb—was accompanied by the plea, "Give them a future." A third photograph, of a woman hunched in the fields, asked, "What does the future hold for the farm worker?" The flyers also named the ticket for governor and lieutenant governor: Aaron Henry and the Reverend Edwin King. Henry was the son of black sharecroppers and a pharmacist from Clarksdale, Mississippi, who, after serving in the military during World War II, received his degree thanks to the G.I. Bill and opened the Fourth Street Drug Store in Jackson with K.W. Walker, a white Mississippian. Ed King was a white Methodist chaplain at Tougaloo College in Jackson and intrinsically involved in the cause for justice. He had grown up in Vicksburg, near Jackson, and attended seminary in Boston, returning to the South in late 1962 to immerse himself in the fight for civil rights.

The mock ballot also included Democratic candidate Paul B. Johnson Jr. and Republican candidate Rubel Phillips. "Ballot boxes were placed in churches, businesses, and homes across the state, and voting took place over a weekend, from Friday to Monday," former SNCC activist Constance Curry wrote in 2011. "Henry and King 'won' the mock election in which more than 80,000 black Mississippians voted. This event showed the country that African Americans would vote if given the chance."

MISSISSIPPI IN THE FALL OF 1963 was a testing ground for the larger civil rights movement. Sellers had not yet ventured into the tumultuous Deep South. Baptized by the violence in Cambridge, Maryland, he was hard at work in the Washington, D.C. area recruiting black student volunteers for the looming voter registration effort in America's poorest, most repressive state. He visited the campuses of the University of Maryland and Morgan State College in Baltimore to talk to students there. SNCC was eager to recruit blacks since many whites already had signed up for the Mississippi Freedom Summer Project at campuses across the country. The uncomfortable truth, noted Carmichael, was that whites could afford to volunteer. Of the black students interested in contributing to the cause, most were poor and many could not dismiss a summer opportunity to earn money to pay for their education. There was, of course, a certain convenient advantage to bringing in hundreds of white volunteers from across the country. Down south, if a black person was arrested or even killed, neither public outcry nor justice ensued. But if a middle-class white student from Boston or Seattle or Los Angeles got into trouble, it was more likely that his senator would intervene or that his local newspaper would cover the story. Thus COFO and SNCC activists stood a better chance of exposing Mississippi's cruel apartheid system to the rest of the world if whites were involved in the fight.

The D.C. leadership crew included Sellers, Courtland Cox, Freedom Rider Hank Thomas, Charles Cobb, Ivanhoe Donaldson and Mike Thelwell, who edited Howard University's student newspaper, The Hilltop. "NAG tried to get people in strategic positions at student organizations," Sellers explained. In his post at the student paper, Thelwell could exercise disproportionate influence, publicizing issues important to the NAG cohort. As the spring semester ended at Howard, the D.C. men (and some women) assumed critical roles—field organizers and project directors—in Mississippi. Carmichael became a district leader responsible for the western stretch of the state, from Holly Springs in the north to Greenwood, encompassing five congressional districts. White students were sent to the southwestern portion of the state, Biloxi and its surroundings, which had a reputation for moderation. Sellers was dispatched to Holly Springs, a relatively calm town seated in Marshall County, a little south of the border with Tennessee. The county's population was 28,000 in 1964. About two-thirds of its residents were African Americans. Farming was the primary occupation and the principle crop was cotton. Much of the land was owned by whites and rented or sharecropped by black farmers.

Overseeing the entire Mississippi effort was SNCC's Bob Moses. Freedom Summer was a culmination of four years of grassroots organizing. Moses had primed the state for this, driven by his acute awareness of inequity as a consequence of deeply rooted national flaws. "Part of the whole idea of the Summer Project was Bob's analysis that the law only covers certain people in America, and it doesn't cover southern blacks," said California volunteer Marshall Ganz. "It covers northern blacks a little bit, and it covers northern whites a whole lot, and so that if you want to bring the law to the South, you have to bring the people who the law covers to the South."

Sellers had decided to go to Mississippi soon after he first learned of the summer project early that year, but he struggled to justify his involvement with his parents. "I had to tell my mom what I would be doing for the summer," he said. "It took a while for my mother to adjust to that." She was deathly afraid, and Sellers had numerous conversations with her in an effort to allay her concerns. He told her about the training and extensive security precautions. He told her he would have a mailing address to make correspondence possible. He told her about his determination and sense of duty, referring to the scholarships he had secured at Howard to help pay tuition and other costs. Since he was responsible for a good portion of the education expenses, he had a right to decide his own fate, he rationalized somewhat unconvincingly. Nevertheless, he expected her to understand and to run interference with his less sympathetic father.

In the course of these conversations with his mother, he asked advice from activist-colleagues about what reassurances he could offer her. "Don't say a lot," they replied.

IN MID-JUNE Cleveland Sellers attended SNCC's orientation meeting for Freedom Summer volunteers held at Western College for Women (now part of Miami University) in Oxford, Ohio. More than 800 volunteers trained at the college campus over two weeks in preparation for civil rights work in Mississippi. The Howard students corralled others from the University of Maryland, Morgan State University, University of the District of Columbia and other campuses and drove straight to Ohio. The D.C. faction, which included Carmichael and Sellers, was the largest all-black group at the orientation meeting. Many of the activists working in Mississippi came north for the conference, including Cornell University student Michael Schwerner and his wife Rita. The Schwerners were in charge of the field office in Meridian, where they had been sent to set up a community center under the auspices of CORE, assisted by Mississippi native James Chaney, a black civil rights worker, and others. A couple of weeks earlier, Schwerner and Chaney had addressed a gathering of blacks at Mt. Zion Methodist Church to urge them to register to vote. The church sat on a rural road east of Philadelphia, Mississippi, and hosted a SNCC Freedom School where children were educated and inculcated in the ways of the freedom movement. Schwerner and Chaney, along with Andrew Goodman of New York, drove to Ohio to join the CORE/SNCC orientation meeting. Soon after arriving, word came on June 17 that Mt. Zion Church had been burnt to the ground—one of 30 black churches in Mississippi firebombed in 1964. They quickly returned to the war zone to investigate. Driving in CORE leader Dave Dennis' blue station wagon,

Schwerner, Chaney and Goodman were stopped on a Mississippi country road, arrested, jailed, then released in the evening and told to leave Neshoba County. Sellers and others speculate that the brief jailing gave the Ku Klux Klan time to plot their next move.

In Oxford, Ohio, word of the disappearance of the three civil rights activists came to Bob Moses on the morning of June 22 as he was addressing the large gathering of volunteers, who until that moment reveled in the novelty of the racially mixed situation and failed to appreciate fully the gravity of what they were about to do. "There were a lot of problems in Oxford, most of them stemming from the innocence of the white volunteers," wrote Sellers in his autobiography, remembering the scene at the orientation meeting. "When we tried to explain the rural South to them, they would nod as if they understood, but their eyes remained blank, uncomprehending. Many of them talked about Mississippi as if it were somehow the same as the romanticized scenes they had read about in *Gone with the Wind*." But now, suddenly, they would be confronted with the disturbing reality.

SNCC staffers interrupted Moses as he was comparing Mississippi's "closed society" to Albert Camus' *The Plague*, which features a town in denial of the infection that's consuming it. After hearing the news, Moses turned back to the volunteers. "Yesterday morning, three of our people left Meridian, Mississippi, to investigate a church burning in Neshoba County," he said, softly. "They haven't come back and we haven't had any word from them." His words carried weight: SNCC and CORE workers were trained well in the art of covert communication with one another, and they strictly obeyed rules that ensured their whereabouts would be known by colleagues. They checked in with field offices at every opportunity. They made certain that co-workers were aware of every move. They understood the importance of leaving a trail. For a day and night to go by without news from Schwerner,

Chaney and Goodman was cause for worry. And the risks of the Summer Project, the violent nature of Mississippi, the human cost of the endeavor now were becoming clear to all those gathered in the college's Peabody Hall.

With the national news focusing on the disappearance of the three civil rights workers, field directors and even more volunteers streamed into Mississippi from Ohio and elsewhere. They faced not one grand mission, but two: simultaneously, they would register voters in preparation for propelling the Mississippi Freedom Democratic Party to Atlantic City at the end of the summer, and they would search for the missing men, pestering state officials and FBI investigators to hurry up and do their jobs, challenging their resistance, stewing all the while on the implications of the crime.

Bob Moses had assigned the Howard students and NAG members leadership roles throughout Mississippi's rural Second Congressional District, so Sellers and his friends felt an immediate and acute responsibility not only for the project but for the safety of all those involved. So when it was decided at the Oxford meeting that somebody should go to the small town of Philadelphia and begin searching for the missing activists, the NAG group—which included Carmichael, Sellers, Charlie Cobb, Ivanhoe Donaldson, Ralph Featherstone and a few others, equipped with overalls and straw hats in order to fit into the rural Mississippi aesthetic—quickly took on the assignment. "We moved out that afternoon," Sellers said, recalling the urgent fear that took hold of everyone in Oxford when they heard about their missing colleagues. They loaded into several cars and took different routes. One car drove south through Memphis; another through Arkansas, another through Alabama. They wanted to avoid forming a conspicuous convoy. By the next morning they were in Mississippi.

Sellers and the others focused initially on a search mission. And on staying alive. He knew it was better to seek shelter in wood-frame houses rather than concrete houses. Wood structures blew apart when explosives detonated, and those inside stood a good chance of surviving since they would be thrown outward, along with the debris. But concrete buildings crashed down upon themselves when bombed. Anyone inside would be buried in the rubble. Sellers learned other lessons: to hold meetings by day and travel about at night when darkness served as a disguise; to stand behind walls, not windows where you could be seen from outside; to keep the lights off, especially when travelling after dark; to use back roads, never the main highways. This war required strategy and caution. Five search teams were assembled, made up of Sellers, Carmichael, Cobb, Featherstone, Donaldson, Gwen Gillon, Donna Moses and a few others.

SNCC workers had canvassed the area identifying places where hostages might be held, or bodies hidden. Sellers' team came upon a farmhouse that it used as a base. The search party, unarmed, remained inside during the day, then explored the surrounding territory by night in a pickup driven by a local, who drove without headlights, only occasionally flashing his parking lights to get his bearings on the dark back roads. "The procedure was always the same," Sellers said. "We'd pile from the truck and fan out. Walking slowly and almost never talking, we searched swamps, creeks, old houses, abandoned barns, orchards, tangled underbrush and unused wells. Most of us used long sticks to probe the many ditches and holes we encountered. When the sticks proved inadequate, as they frequently did, we had to feel about in the dark with our hands and feet." The search team did not use flashlights; they wore nothing reflective. "We were on our own in the wilderness." They encountered plenty of snakes. When they found a well, someone would toss in a small stone. If they heard a thud, or nothing at all, rather than a telltale "plunk," one of searchers would lean over the edge and sniff in order to detect rotting flesh. On the third day, they gave up their quest. Law enforcement authorities probably had caught wind of the effort and the black owner of the farmhouse where they were staying was getting nervous.

AS THE FEDERAL INVESTIGATION ramped up, SNCC work returned their attention to the political campaign. Sellers made his way to Holly Springs to help coordinate efforts in five counties that, together, produced the largest number of registered voters in the state and the largest delegation at the Democratic Convention in Atlantic City later that summer. He settled into a white frame house situated not far from Rust College, a historically black liberal arts institution. The living room became the official meeting space; four bedrooms accommodated staffers and volunteers. "We got there and there were already some students who had arrived while we were in Philadelphia," he recalled. "The very next day we had a meeting, and started talking about assignments, rules and regulations for safety and communication. We talked about the importance of getting applications for the Mississippi Freedom Democratic Party, and gathering as many as we could for the convention." Right away, he and his team began collecting evidence of political fraud and delivering materials to SNCC's "Watch Line" repository in Atlanta.

Sellers worked closely with Ivanhoe Donaldson who, the following year, would assist Julian Bond in his bid for the Georgia Statehouse and later would manage the political ascent of Marion Barry in Washington, D.C. In Mississippi, Donaldson already was a SNCC veteran and assigned to be project director in Holly Springs. Nineteen-year-old Sellers was assistant project director and spent most of his time out of the office coordinating voter registration, running Freedom Schools and organizing for the Mississippi Freedom Democratic Party throughout Marshall

County. Every two or three weeks, he arranged a Freedom Day when activists brought as many people as possible into Holly Springs to get them registered to vote. Donaldson was a no-nonsense leader who enforced strict rules and expected a disciplined team. He forbade interracial romantic entanglements and insisted on hard work. "I intend for us to have the best goddamn project in the state," he told his staff. "We're going to register more voters than anyone else, have the most efficient Freedom Schools and the best MFDP precincts."

Thousands were registered in and around Holly Springs alone, Sellers said. His office ultimately succeeded in registering as many as 70,000 black voters. The office also operated three Freedom Schools where Featherstone and Cobb taught, along with four teachers from Massachusetts. Holly Springs was by no means violence-free. A couple of churches in the area were firebombed by Klansmen, and a pair of African-American SNCC workers were involved in a mysterious head-on collision that killed one of them, Wayne Yancey—an episode that angered and traumatized Sellers and his colleagues. Sellers himself had a few close calls with the law, one resulting in a high-speed chase from Oxford to Holly Springs. But generally violence was isolated and limited in the northern part of the state. Oxford, where the University of Mississippi was located, sat about 30 miles to the south, and the college town acted as a tempering force, and even produced a number of young people sympathetic to the civil rights cause.

In late July, 44 days after the disappearance of Schwerner, Chaney and Goodman, the FBI found their bodies and began to piece together the mystery of their murder. On their way back to Meridian after being released from jail on June 21, they had been intercepted by Klansmen in two cars, shot and killed (Chaney, the African American, was tortured first), then buried in an earthen dam at Old Jolly Farm. When Sellers got the news, he fell ill.

"What I remember is the excruciating pain it caused in my stomach," he wrote. "The pain, which remained for several days and nights, plagued my mind until it was impossible for me to rest or to forget what had been done to those three innocent men."

IN THE MIDST of this human drama, SNCC staff was accumulating piles of documentation describing voter suppression, harassment and other racist efforts that had guaranteed the election of white delegates to the upcoming Democratic Convention. It had been a grueling summer in Mississippi, fraught with risk and responsibility. Whites resisted the influx of "outside agitators," but so did many blacks. Black churches often kept their doors closed to organizers; black households often rejected pleas to participate in the political process. The young volunteers were occasionally looked upon with skepticism and fear. Many of the poor blacks who did obey failed to pass the registration tests designed to keep them powerless. Many lost their jobs as a result of their efforts. The organizers, including Sellers, understood the consequences, intended and unintended, and knew they were complicit in causing added hardship to the lives of these rural families. They pursued their goals with respect, kindness and determination, but not without a constant awareness that they were endangering themselves and others. Local whites solidified into a hegemonic bloc, resisting with force every attempt by "invaders" to break the system of oppression. They armed themselves, police and average citizen alike, forming an informal statewide militia ready to engage in battle with nonviolent activists. Citizens' Councils enforced Jim Crow and colluded with local and state governments. Hundreds were arrested. Even the most modest gesture by blacks—a quiet march whose participants held up small American flags—was brutally disrupted. Police snatched the flags from each marcher, as if to say, "You are not an American citizen." The Klan worked diligently to excite the "persecuted people" of Anglo-Saxon descent forced to endure this assault from foreign invaders. "We are in the midst of the long, hot summer of agitation promised to the innocent people of Mississippi by the savage blacks and their Communist masters," the United Klans of America declared in a July 4 publication. During the search for the bodies of the three civil rights workers, many whites had insisted that all this hubbub over Schwerner, Chaney and Goodman was a lot of hot air. The trio probably had run scared to Cuba, they said. The allegations were just a hoax thrust upon innocent whites.

Julian Bond, SNCC's communications director based in Atlanta, and civil rights activists in Washington, D.C., tried to interest the national press in the large-scale volunteer voter registration drive and political organizing underway in Mississippi and the vehement resistance by whites, with little success. The press had been following the case of the missing workers, which ultimately would help instigate President Johnson to push for the Voting Rights Act, first introduced in the Senate in March 1965 and signed into law on August 6. But the larger story concerning Mississippi's entrenched racism, Klan terrorism, voter suppression, and attempts by COFO and SNCC to make the state more democratic and inclusive was given short shrift.

BY LATE SUMMER, the Mississippi activists had amassed boxes and boxes of evidence in the murder of the three civil rights workers, reclaimed the burnt-out Ford station wagon the trio had been driving, assembled a large delegation, registered tens of thousands to vote and prepared to convene in Atlantic City for the Democratic Convention, August 24-27. Sellers was responsible for transforming the mangled hulk of the automobile into an outdoor exhibit so the world could view a terrible emblem of Jim Crow violence. "We took up [to Atlantic City] a number of people who had never been out of the state of Mississippi in their lives," Sellers said. "Some had never been out of the county that they grew up in. And here they were, going north to represent their families and their friends and their party and their county and their precinct. And it was just a good feeling that here we are, we're on the threshold of bringing about change."

Back in Denmark, Sellers' father worried. He was aware of what was happening; television delivered the harsh reality into his living room, and Cleveland Sellers Jr. kept his parents apprised of the situation, more or less, through letters. On one or two occasions, the elder Sellers wrote back.

My Dear Son,

I received your letter and enjoyed reading, The motel plan is waiting for you.

Please come home you have been away long enough. It time for you to [return to school]. I can't sleep. I am always thinking about you. I have been working . . . for long time.

If you want to fly home call me. I will make all arrangement.

Please let me see you Thanksgiving.

We are planning to see Gwen. Please don't be a Dead Hero.

Your Dady C.L.

6   ATLANTIC CITY

PART OF CLEVE SELLERS' JOB in the summer of 1964 was
signing up members of the Mississippi Freedom Democratic
Party, a rival party to the Democratic Party in Mississippi, or
Dixiecrats, who held fiercely to a segregationist ideology and were
complicit in the marginalization of black voters. By the time of
the Democratic Convention in Atlantic City in late August, the
racially-integrated MFDP had 80,000 members who intended
to replace the officially-recognized Democratic Party delegates.
Sellers' efforts from Holly Springs had borne fruit: he and his team
of organizers had signed up 30,000 people as members of MFDP,
more than any of the other SNCC and CORE platoons operating

in the state. He was tasked with transporting to Atlantic City boxes of documentation on voter suppression, the damaged car used by Schwerner, Chaney and Goodman, as well as the salvaged bell of the firebombed Mt. Zion Methodist Church, which had become a symbol of the horror taking place in Mississippi. He rented a flatbed truck for the purpose and drove in a small convoy to New Jersey via Denmark where he stopped for a couple of hours to see his parents and have a meal.

The delegation spent the first few days in Atlantic City setting up an encampment on the boardwalk, with the burned remains of the car elevated for display, the bell and huge banners with the images of Schwerner, Chaney and Goodman emblazoned on them. The Freedom Singers were on hand. MFDP activists, including Sellers, Bob Moses, Ivanhoe Donaldson, Stokely Carmichael and H. Rap Brown, lobbied seated Democratic Party delegates, arguing the case for representative government. "We were optimistic because we knew we were the real representatives of the people," Sellers said. "I had real hopes we were on the verge of a breakthrough."

BUT IT WAS NOT the young male activists in Mississippi who grabbed the nation's attention in Atlantic City. Fannie Lou Hamer, a matronly and dynamic figure who had worked as a sharecropper and knew Mississippi's brand of oppression intimately, stepped forward to become the voice of oppressed black residents of her home state. Throughout 1963-64 she had helped galvanize activists with her forceful determination, faith and fervent embrace of the diversity she hoped her home state might one day celebrate. Her activism had led to an arrest the year before and a brutal beating in jail. It was the sort of violent attack meant to strip her of her dignity. Though forever traumatized by it, Hamer's self-respect, and her respect for other good people, only burned brighter. Older than the volunteers and SNCC staff, she gained an important place in the organization and assumed the role of vice chairwoman of the Mississippi Freedom Democratic Party. Hamer believed that civil rights had to be a multiracial fight, that its goal was not just integration and equality but cooperation, and the Summer Project was evidence that this could come to pass. Hamer quickly became one of the project's lead spokespeople, and her role at the fore took her all the way to New Jersey where she was designated to testify before the convention's Credentials Committee.

The essential argument MFDP members made at the convention was simple: the regular Democratic Party was disloyal to democracy, the Dixiecrats were disloyal to the party and the Freedom Democrats were able to correct the moral-political imbalance. In Bob Moses' words, the gathering faced an opportunity "to lay the foundation for building another base." For many of the MFDP activists, this was the first time they had participated in something this significant. They had never left their Mississippi county, let alone the state, Sellers noted. Here they were, suddenly, with a loud collective voice, arguing for democratic justice—and being heard. On August 22, Hamer testified before the Credentials Committee, her speech televised nationally. She spoke of being forced to leave the farm on which she was a sharecropper after registering to vote in 1962. She told the committee about her wrongful arrest, imprisonment and beating. "All of this is on account of we want to register, to become first-class citizens," she said. "And if the Freedom Democratic Party is not seated now, I question America. Is this America, the land of the free and the home of the brave, where we have to sleep with our telephones off the hooks because our lives be threatened daily, because we want to live as decent human beings, in America?" The audience was riveted. The MFDP delegation was elated. The moral message was delivered loud and clear.

Sellers thought the world of Hamer and wasn't surprised by her powerful statement. "We met at one of the staff meetings we used to have (in Mississippi), probably on a monthly basis," he said, recalling her charisma and moral authority. "You could feel her presence. It was clear that her experiences were very rich and that she had suffered." She had visited the Oxford orientation meeting to speak to the volunteers about what they could expect to find in her home state, telling them of the daily humiliations endured by blacks. "There were not that many SNCC leaders in Mississippi, so I got to know Fannie Lou Hamer pretty well," Sellers said. "We traveled around to various projects together." And nearly everywhere they went attention was focused on her.

Soon after Hamer began to speak at the convention, President Lyndon Johnson, aware of the testimony underway, became livid and called an impromptu press conference to which the networks cut away. He wanted Hamer off the air. That night, though, the networks replayed her testimony in full, and American viewers everywhere glimpsed briefly the human dimension of state-sponsored terrorism against their fellow citizens. The next day, the Oregon delegation announced it had voted 20-0 to replace the current Mississippi delegation with representatives of the Freedom Democratic Party. Others began to voice their support for the switch, too. Sellers and the rest of the Mississippi activists were beginning to feel confident, openly expressing their optimism. They all convened later that day for a debriefing. "I don't think that if this issue gets to the floor of that convention that they could possibly turn us down," Moses told his colleagues. "I don't see how they possibly could do it if they really understand what's at stake."

SELLERS MOSTLY REMAINED with the MFDP delegation and SNCC colleagues, spending the bulk of his time in Atlantic City on the boardwalk where he and the others organized protests, distributed literature about Mississippi's discriminatory practices, presented the Freedom Singers to passersby and kept an eye on the convention schedule to ensure the delegates—Hamer, the Reverand Ed King, Mississippi NAACP President Aaron Henry and others—didn't miss anything important. Meetings, like the one with Moses, were held in one of the hotels or on a pier nearby. The MFDP team stayed in a hotel, seven or eight people per room, with several climbing into sleeping bags on the floor. Sellers and his colleagues followed Hamer's live testimony from the hotel. "We kept up with everything that was going on."

And they understood the significance of the moment. The Dixiecrats, a hugely influential bloc within the party and in Washington, D.C., threatened to throw their support behind the presidential candidate Barry Goldwater and shift their political allegiance to the Republican Party. Johnson understood the stakes, too. He knew that he was going to lose the South sooner or later, especially as he advanced John F. Kennedy's civil rights agenda— something he repeatedly promised to do. But he wasn't prepared to lose the South yet. First he wanted to secure his re-election. So Johnson sent in vice presidential nominee and avowed liberal Hubert Humphrey to stop the MFDP in its tracks, "to keep our convention united." LBJ worked the phones; Humphrey and United Automobile Workers president Walter Reuther met with the upstart Freedom Democrats to see if a deal could be worked out. Soon, the whole Mississippi contingency began to hear about the backpedaling. One woman admitted that she was withdrawing her support because her husband's candidacy for a judgeship now was under threat.

On Tuesday afternoon, the crisis reached its peak. Walter Mondale, who would replace Humphrey in the U.S. Senate later that year, called a meeting with MFDP representatives and others in the nearby Shelburne Hotel and offered a compromise: The delegation would be invited into the convention hall as spectators and the Freedom Democrat's Aaron Henry and Ed King would be granted at-large seats and the right to vote. Meanwhile, as the two sides discussed the matter at the hotel, delegates inside the convention center were calling for a vote. Joseph Rauh, attorney for the MFDP and head of its D.C. delegation, a man with deep connections to the Democratic Party, tried to filibuster before the Credentials Committee, asking for a roll call, speaking at length on anything that came to mind, but he could not force a long-enough pause in the proceedings. The Freedom Democrats were rejected, a result that nevertheless did not satisfy the Dixiecrats, who walked out. When the MFDP negotiators emerged from the hotel room, they were confronted by a curious press corps: What did they think of the vote? Mystification gave way to a profound sense of betrayal. "It was just complete manipulation and cynicism," Moses said.

Moses was not alone in feeling double-crossed. His anger was shared among all the SNCC, CORE and MFDP people. Sellers said it was a major turning point, both for him personally and for the movement in general. "I simply lost my innocence and began to understand the magnitude of what we were trying to do," he said. "I learned so much about the resilience and fortitude of ordinary citizens under the oppression that African Americans were going through then." Simple, courageous citizens of Mississippi, denied their rights, fought their way to the Democratic Party Convention, lost the immediate battle, but knew that the war would continue to demand vigilance and sacrifice. *Tomorrow will be a new day*, they told the young activists of SNCC. "That was a lesson that most of us learned fast," Sellers said.

When Humphrey was asked by the media about the resolution, he said, "I think it was a victory for the forces of reason and I think it was a victory for the Democratic Party. I think it was a victory for our country." The next day, the activists met to further discuss the matter. Many important liberals, black and white, joined the meeting to encourage the group to accept the deal. Martin Luther King, Roy Wilkins and Walter Reuther called it a modest victory. Oregon's Rep. Edith Green and Sen. Wayne Morse also supported the arrangement. It was better than nothing, they argued. But the young Mississippi activists were unswayed. They voted to reject what was a merely symbolic gesture. Fannie Lou Hamer concurred with them: "We didn't come all the way up here to compromise for no more than we'd gotten here. We didn't come all this way for no two seats when everyone's tired," she proclaimed. When someone asked her why she felt compelled to continue the fight, Hamer replied, "All my life I've been sick and tired. Now I'm sick and tired of being sick and tired." She came to understand that the white power structure was not going to give up political control willingly. Appeals to moral conscience were not enough.

On the last day of the convention, after the Dixiecrats had abandoned their seats, MFDP representatives made their way into the hall with tickets provided by sympathetic participants and confronted Johnson who appeared behind the podium to give a speech. They wanted him to know that they understood what he had done; they knew the liberals had offended democracy and justice in order to consolidate power. They had come to the convention as believers in the institutions of American government, bringing with them the testimonials and the debris of racism. They made a strong case for fairness, even winning a degree of support on the floor. But it was not enough to preach the truth and appeal to the better angels of their fellow Americans. It was not enough to share stories of ducking bullets in order to secure the right to vote. It was not enough to point to the placards displaying the faces of three martyrs to the cause. Even in Atlantic City, the

Klan's presence was felt, Sellers said. Even there, the civil rights activists, unarmed, always were on their guard, always were fearful of dangerous encounters after dark, always clustered together in groups and looked forward to putting the experience behind them.

ONE MIGHT CONSIDER the Atlantic City fiasco in another light, though: despite the double dealing and bad faith that resulted in such profound disillusionment, Fannie Lou Hamer and her cohort of MFDP activists managed an important victory (even if they unwittingly set the stage for future partisan rancor). They helped to excise the Dixiecrats from the Democratic Party and prompted a significant political realignment that would define Democrats as advocates for working-class and middle-class Americans for several generations. But in doing so, they assigned the South to the Republicans for decades to come. To be sure, other forces contributed to the upheaval, such as Goldwater's rhetoric, Nixon's Southern Strategy and the rise of the conservative media, including William Buckley's National Review, founded in 1955. But it was Hamer and Sellers and Carmichael and Moses and the many others who trekked to New Jersey from Mississippi that summer who lanced the rot within the Democratic Party and accelerated the process of realignment.

At the end of that August, however, the activists thought little of tectonic shifts and mostly of their immense disappointment. "We left Atlantic City with a profound sense of betrayal," Sellers said. If the official electoral process doesn't work, what next? Disillusionment permeated the delegation, as well as the black and white volunteers and SNCC organizers who had worked so hard in Mississippi, who had risked their lives, who had lost friends and colleagues, to achieve some measure of political progress and enfranchisement. "The challenge was very significant because it made us realize that the whole conspiracy was not just a conspiracy of the South," wrote H. Rap Brown in his autobiography. "It was a conspiracy of the nation. The MFDP challenge not only pointed up the total lack of power black people had, but it also showed that even when you're right, you lose."

Even in defeat, Sellers and the other activists gained insights that would inform their future decisions and political thinking. The convention marked an ideological break with past efforts to integrate public spaces and push for equality. Going forward, the movement would focus on self-preservation and self-determination. No longer would its leaders expect white officials and politicians to sympathize with the cause or seek to negotiate and compromise. This was indeed a new day.

"We were angry, but what we learned was a very good lesson about power and politics and the party structure," Sellers said. "Morality was an ideal, but it wasn't something that was practiced. I recognized that we had gone as far as we could. We were securing the right to vote. And then when we had all of the civil rights leadership turn on us, [and] when you find out that the Democratic Party had turned on us, there was a certain amount of reality that kicked in....It was like the poor people of Mississippi and us against the whole universe."

7 IN BETRAYAL'S WAKE

AFTER THE INTENSE EXPERIENCES in Mississippi and Atlantic City, Sellers returned to Denmark for a week's rest. He was physically tired and emotionally battered. Political betrayal was bad enough, but Sellers also had endured the deaths of four colleagues, which tried his nerves. At home, his parents and sister made their inquiries and Sellers did his best to share information and calm their concerns. But there was a disconnect: worried about his safety, they wondered why he persisted, when he would return to school, whether there wasn't something different he might do. Observing the civil rights movement from a distance, they marveled at the circumstances that drove these young men and women—that drove Cleveland Sellers Jr.—to choose to fight. But this was no choice, not anymore. Sellers had too much invested. He was part of a warrior brigade still immersed in confrontation with an enemy both tangible and philosophical. It was impossible to turn away now. But maybe his family did appreciate his condition, perhaps they detected the inexorable political change underway; perhaps, too, they sensed that the movement had reached a decisive moment, one that would lead to a new kind of confrontation and to more violence. When after his short visit home Sellers prepared himself for the drive back to Mississippi, his father followed him outside and extended his hand. A look of tender concern flashed across his face. "Take care of yourself, boy," he whispered, choking up.

While Sellers recuperated at home, then returned to Holly Springs to continue party registration work (albeit with a smaller staff), other SNCC workers, including Bob Moses, were afforded an opportunity by Harry Belafonte to travel to Guinea in West Africa as guests of President Sékou Touré. Guinea and other countries in the region were shedding their colonial past and entering a post-revolutionary phase. There, the American activists witnessed black people in charge, running the machinery of government, controlling the security apparatus and carrying themselves with the pride of those free to determine their own destinies. It was the first time many in the group had stepped outside of the U.S., and the impression made by the trip was one contributing factor in the shift of the civil rights movement toward an emphasis on self-determination and black empowerment. The civil rights slogan "One Man, One Vote" in fact had been borrowed from Ghana. If Africans could be self-sufficient, then surely African Americans could achieve the same. The evidence was beginning to pile up: organizational success in the South, examples of black rule in Africa, the unreliability of existing power structures in the U.S. and a growing international consensus in support of the civil rights movement all were beginning to influence the philosophy behind the freedom fight.

What's more, activists were increasingly aware of developments abroad, such as the crisis in the Middle East, the war in Vietnam, Cold War confrontations, freedom movements in the Caribbean and the disastrous effect of apartheid in South Africa. Long-debated issues, such as the role of whites in the movement and the goals of inclusiveness and integration, were generating renewed scrutiny, except now the general awareness and experience of the movement's participants had evolved and the status of the effort in the U.S. had changed. The Civil Rights Act was signed into law by President Johnson on July 2, 1964, and momentum was gathering in support of the Voting Rights Act, which would become law on August 6 the following year. These legislative victories were among the developments signaling that the movement's enfranchisement phase was drawing to an end. The law had changed, but not the attitudes and behavior of many whites in the South, and not the conditions of the urban poor in the North.

IN HOLLY SPRINGS, Sellers discovered he had become project director. Ivanhoe Donaldson had been called to SNCC headquarters in Atlanta to assume a new position. Sellers, fully immersed in the movement since the Cambridge episode, had given up on the idea of returning to Howard to finish his undergraduate studies. "I decided to quit school once I got to Mississippi and had to deal with Schwerner, Goodman and Chaney," he said. "I met Ben Chaney, James' little brother. When they found the body it completely destroyed him. He worshipped his older brother [who] was a hero to him.... That made what I was doing, and what we were doing, a lot more important than going back and getting your degree in engineering and being window dressing for corporations."

He spent a few months trying to re-energize earlier voter registration efforts with an eye toward strengthening the MFDP and positioning it for another campaign. He was working within a transformed organization. Before Freedom Summer, SNCC was lean and mean and mostly black. By the fall of 1964 it was hundreds strong, mostly white, with offices throughout Mississippi and Alabama, headquarters in Atlanta, a fleet of vehicles and a significant budget. Its leaders were struggling to manage this new reality even as they devised new strategies, identified new initiatives and reacted to developments on the ground. In Holly Springs, Sellers continued to organize for the Mississippi Freedom Democratic Party. He and his colleagues had not yet thrown in the towel; they figured they might rally the troops and launch another challenge. They kept registering voters, mentoring young people and challenging recalcitrant officials struggling to maintain the old order.

SNCC leaders in Atlanta organized a three-day staff meeting in Waveland, Mississippi, at the end of November. The reorganization had begun. The meeting produced a critical strategic decision: Since poor blacks could not rely on existing power structures to solve their problems, independent political organizations would have to be formed to represent the interests of the marginalized. The gathering drew not only Sellers and the rest of the leadership team but the many volunteers who joined the Freedom Summer campaign and then decided to stay on. Executive Director James Forman had invited anyone interested to submit position papers addressing aspects of the movement and recommending courses of action. Casey Hayden and Mary King produced a paper concerning sexism within SNCC, which confused many in attendance. Wasn't the main issue racism? Judy Richardson noted the general chaos and discord and became concerned. "What I remember most about this meeting was the almost constant tension and confusion," she said. To eat at the retreat one had to produce a meal ticket—only available to staff members. People were being turned away if they didn't have a pass, and this heightened the acrimony.

"We were now at the point of arguing about *meal tickets*, but only because we couldn't get our minds around all those other issues that were tearing us apart."

Attendees debated the changing nature of the movement and what it demanded of SNCC. This was a fight about black liberation and empowerment after all. Could SNCC forge ahead effectively as an integrated group with so many white volunteers? Or should black leaders draw a line in the sand? Was the goal for blacks to find a way to function within an imperfect society, or for a mixed collection of activists to establish a new model for a post-racial America? Arguments erupted over whether SNCC's decentralized structure could be sustained. Forman proposed establishing a strong executive committee in order to shore up the group. Now that the organization was larger, perhaps it required some degree of hierarchical authority, some said. *Someone* had to keep track of the assets; *someone* had to set the agenda.

Sellers, still coping with profound disillusionment because of what transpired at the Democratic National Convention, was determined to push forward, thanks in some measure to Fannie Lou Hamer's persistence and her faith in the freedom movement. "Fannie Lou Hamer uplifted everyone," he recalled. "In spite of the disappointment and heartbreak, she was strong enough, and had enough courage, to say what it was, and what she didn't like about it. 'We've been fighting too long to give up now,' she said." As for *how* to forge ahead, well, that would require more rigorous control of SNCC's resources, according to Sellers.

THE CONFUSION WAS NOT settled in Waveland; it persisted through 1965, causing some of SNCC's prominent leaders— those who joined the organization early and became known for their pragmatism, adherence to nonviolence and determination

to seek reform from within systems—to leave. In 1965, Julian
Bond launched a bid for the Georgia House of Representatives.
Bob Moses, appearing at a SNCC staff meeting in early 1965,
announced he was changing his name to Robert Parris and depart-
ing for Africa where he would be a teacher. The organization was
bigger than ever and suddenly unsure of its purpose and agenda.
The passage of the Civil Rights Act and Voting Rights Act further
destabilized SNCC, seeming to undermine its mission. After all,
weren't these the sort of victories SNCC had been fighting for?
"When the federal government passed bills that supposedly supported black voting and outlawed public segregation, SNCC lost
the initiative in these areas," Sellers wrote in his memoir.

Many years later, Sellers would describe four main phases of
SNCC: the start-up period of mass action and civil disobedience,
informed by the sit-ins and Freedom Rides; the enfranchisement
phase, focused on voter education and registration as well as political action (especially in Mississippi); the empowerment phase,
characterized by independent political organizing, the transfer of
tactics developed in the South to northern urban centers and the
rise of Black Power and the internationalist phase, which featured
a broader critique of oppression worldwide and the final dissolu-
tion of SNCC. "I also would make the argument that each of these
divisions represents a generation at SNCC," Bond said, "and that
the people who came to the first generation, the sit-in generation,
are very different than the people who came to the fourth.... They
think about things differently."

The organization became increasingly radical during the second half of the 1960s, associating itself with liberation struggles
elsewhere, reserving the right to use violence as a response to violence (at least theoretically), and distinguishing black Americans
from other ethnic groups. Sellers, who joined the movement
during the enfranchisement phase, rose in the ranks during the

empowerment period and embraced the new radicalism whose public face was, primarily, his friend Stokely Carmichael, followed by H. Rap Brown. "Since the liberal consensus was done by '65, anything that happened after '65 was a struggle between the radical approach to an economic program and a moderate approach," said Bob Zellner, who would be asked two years later to separate himself from the black cause, along with other white organizers. "And that's when the liberals left; that's when Black Power came into its own. And you had someone like Cleve who had bridged that. He had been in on the integration stage of things and now he was still in a strong leadership position after '65 when the liberal consensus had broken down. And we never were able to get the kind of revolutionary follow-up. After the liberal consensus fell apart, the government… was able to use narrow nationalism as a way of keeping a revolutionary coalition from occurring.… And Cleve was right there. So he was dealing with all of the craziness of the narrow nationalists while trying to develop an analysis of radical nationalism, black nationalism."

After the Waveland meeting, SNCC introduced the Mississippi Challenge, an effort with two purposes in mind. One was to show the new Congress that the Mississippi delegation was unjustly elected and should be denied their seats in the House of Representatives. Evidence of voter suppression was abundant, of course, and was used to make the case. The other purpose was to show blacks that petitioning the authorities—that playing the game whose rules had been devised by those interested in obtaining and maintaining power—would do little to change the status quo, for it was expected that the Mississippi Challenge would fail in Congress. It did (though a surprising number of congressmen, 143, voted to deny seats to the Mississippi contingent during a roll-call vote).

* ❀ *

ON JANUARY 2, 1965, two days before Congress' roll-call
vote, Martin Luther King announced that the Southern Christian
Leadership Conference (SCLC) would lead a voter registration
effort and big march in Selma, Alabama, a hot seat of racial unrest
and white resistance. This caused some consternation among
SNCC staffers who recognized the potential for internecine conflict. SCLC had a reputation for high-profile, attention-grab-
bing, short-term efforts that might turn public opinion against
Southern oppressors; it did not have SNCC's experience with
long-term, grassroots organizing, and SNCC leaders often felt
that while they toiled and sacrificed, King reaped the glory. The
Selma announcement made some in SNCC, including Sellers, feel
a little like King was usurping territory already occupied and tactics already employed by their own team. SNCC members saw no
other choice but to join the effort, though they did so reluctantly
and tentatively.

On February 4, at the invitation of SNCC's Fay Bellamy and
Silas Norman, Malcolm X delivered a short speech to a crowd that
filled the small Brown Chapel AME Church in Selma, condemn-
ing the Johnson administration for failing to protect the voting
rights of workers in Alabama with federal troops. The tension and
hostility in Selma, palpable for months, foretold a violent erup-
tion. King was in jail, along with Ralph Abernathy, after attempting three days earlier to lead a march of about 300 people wanting
to register to vote. He was not present when Malcolm, who had
recently severed his ties to the Nation of Islam, gave his speech.
Malcolm, referring to the slavery era's obsequious house Negro
and defiant field Negro in an analogy for how blacks and whites
might relate to one another, said, "If I can't live in the house as a
human being, I'm praying for that house to blow down, I'm praying for a strong wind to come along. But if we are all going to live
as human beings, as brothers, then I am for a society of human

beings that can practice brotherhood." Some in Selma had worried that Malcolm would denounce nonviolence and sow division, especially after he had dismissed suggestions that his speech could do more harm than good. It turned out that his critics had little to worry about. "I'm not intending to try and stir you up and make you do something that you wouldn't have done anyway," he told those gathered in the pews. "I pray that God will bless you in everything that you do."

He told Coretta Scott King he hoped his presence in Selma, and his message of self-defense, would help the cause. "If white people realize what the alternative is, perhaps they will be more willing to hear Dr. King." About a week later, Sellers attended SNCC's staff meeting in Atlanta. Executive Director James Forman argued at the meeting that a voter registration campaign required extended commitment and support from the federal government, which SCLC seemed to lack. SNCC, Foreman said, should plot its own course. In the end, SNCC declared its lukewarm support of the Selma effort and agreed to provide a small degree of logistical aid. Work in Mississippi slackened or was put on hold. Attention turned to Alabama, especially Lowndes County, where in 1965 none of its black citizens—80 percent of the population—was registered to vote. SNCC staff members at the meeting discussed many other issues, including their opposition to the Vietnam War and organizational concerns. "We were trying to assess what [SNCC] people were doing, what was going on in the projects and how we could shape those projects so they could be more effective," Sellers recalled. "It was about being more technical in our approach to things." Attendees debated philosophical and practical matters, and ultimately a consensus emerged: the organization needed someone methodical and analytical and strategic, someone like Sellers, to oversee its multitude of active projects in several states. Sellers was named program director.

He was briefly in Albany, Georgia, checking on a project when on February 21 he received a call from the SNCC office in Atlanta informing him of Malcolm X's assassination in Harlem by three members of the Nation of Islam. Sadness washed over him. "I thought the world of Malcolm," he said. Sellers, who first met Malcolm in 1963, believed that encounters with pragmatic students of the South had influenced the militant Muslim from the North—sensitized him to the complexities of the movement. In the last year of his life, the firebrand had given way to the humanist. Young people in the Deep South had helped make it happen. "The most important thing about Malcolm was his ability to change," Sellers said. "Some of us live our entire lives and we don't make the first change."

Sellers felt the loss acutely, but his practical nature came to the fore, as it always seemed to do, affording him the ability to assess the social and political impacts of tragedy and loss. "I was just very distressed and frustrated, because I thought that we had begun to [have an] impact on Malcolm, and Malcolm was beginning to make the shift, and was beginning to see not civil rights, but human rights, as being something that he could be involved in, and those human rights organizations in the South he could be involved in, over the question of voter registration," Sellers said during an interview for the TV documentary "Eyes on the Prize II." "Malcolm had said that he would assist with voter registration. We even had a kind of commitment from Malcolm to go into Mississippi to speak to the Mississippi Freedom Democratic Party. And we saw a growth on both parts. We saw Malcolm growing. We saw SNCC growing."

Sellers would represent SNCC, along with John Lewis and James Forman, at the February 27 funeral in Harlem. In Faith Temple of the Church of God in Christ, Sellers took a seat close to the front. In turn, he viewed the body. Sellers, ill-prepared for the wintry cold of New York City, was wearing only a light sports jacket. He decided not to go to the cemetery.

A FEW WEEKS LATER, mass demonstrations in Selma achieved the desired effect of casting a spotlight on police brutality and endemic racism. This would be the penultimate big march of the movement, one that was to culminate at the state capital in Montgomery where participants would demand access to the polls and equal treatment under the law. SNCC Chairman John Lewis was determined to participate, and he wanted his organization to play a central role, despite objections raised by colleagues. The Selma-to-Montgomery march was planned for March 7; participants refused to heed warnings from law enforcement to stay home. As the procession crossed the Edmund Pettus Bridge, hundreds of marchers were beaten back by state troopers armed with nightsticks, tear gas and "nausea" gas, and by a horse-mounted sheriff's posse brandishing bullwhips and electric cattle prods. About 90 people were injured in the confrontation, 17 seriously enough to require hospitalization, including Lewis whose skull had been fractured. The episode was televised, horrifying much of the nation and quickly earning the nickname "Bloody Sunday."

Sellers had been in Jackson, four hours west, attending an MFDP meeting when he got news of the violence and Lewis' injuries. He and several colleagues, including Willie Ricks, Cynthia Washington and George Green, jumped into their cars and rushed to Selma. They had not supported Lewis when he announced his intention to march, but now that things had gone awry, they would join the protest, fueled by anger and a lingering sense of solidarity.

Retreating back to Brown Chapel, King and other organizers decided to march again two days later, but this time they would try to obtain a court order and protection from federal authorities.

Before this could be accomplished, however, Judge Frank Minis Johnson Jr. issued a restraining order, prohibiting the marchers from crossing the Dallas County line. King did not want to aggravate Johnson, a sympathetic figure who tended to favor the legal arguments made by defenders of the movement, so for the second Selma march, King led the procession of about 2,500, which included Sellers and the SNCC contingency, to the bridge in a symbolic gesture meant to pay tribute to those injured two days earlier. During a planning meeting held at Brown Chapel AME Church, Ricks had argued forcefully that the marchers should disregard the court order, challenging the authorities. His heated rhetoric, with which Sellers sympathized, angered King, who chastised him: "You are not Dr. King, *I* am Dr. King," he said.

State troopers were at the foot of the bridge to receive the protestors, but Gov. George Wallace ordered the troopers to pull out, leaving the way clear for the marchers. Some believed it was a trap set by Wallace to force the judge into jailing King for contempt of the injunction should the civil rights leader cross the bridge and the county line. But the ploy failed; no line was crossed. King led the marchers back to Selma.

Jim Forman, opposed to these tactics, went ahead to Montgomery, while other SNCC leaders, including Sellers, stayed put. On March 16, Johnson ruled in favor of the marchers, declaring they had a constitutional right to protest en masse and seek redress from their government representatives. People streamed into Selma to join the effort. SNCC leaders, outraged by the recent events, threw their full support behind the third and final intercity procession. On March 25, as many as 25,000 protestors, who were protected by 2,000 U.S. Army soldiers, 1,900 Alabama National Guardsmen under federal command and many FBI agents and federal marshals, walked peacefully from Selma to the statehouse in Montgomery to confront Wallace.

The Selma campaign left Sellers with a bad taste in his mouth. He and others in SNCC argued at the time that the costs outweighed the benefits, that it was all a lot of show with little substantive gain. SNCC, after all, was used to incremental grassroots results, not grand made-for-television statements. They went along because John Lewis had his skull bashed in, because many had been brutally attacked, because Wallace had once again exposed his racist misogyny, because Alabama had proven to be an intransigent problem that demanded direct action, because, in Sellers words, "We were in too far to back out." Freedom Summer had led to an uncertain winter for SNCC, which in turn gave way to the tumultuous Selma campaign that revealed and widened fractures within the movement.

Selma was viewed ambivalently by some of its participants, but there is no question it profoundly influenced the course of events at the time. President Johnson now was inescapably embroiled in the civil rights protests, and began to modify his rhetoric in support of voting reform and economic justice. He even adopted the most famous motto of the movement, "We shall overcome," using it in a March 15 speech to Congress. The Voting Rights Act was introduced by the White House to Congress on March 17 and passed the Senate overwhelmingly on May 26. The House approved its version of the bill on July 9, after weeks of intense debate. Johnson signed the act into law on August 6. Five days later, riots erupted in Los Angeles' Watts neighborhood. The fight for freedom and justice entered its new phase during which SNCC would fracture, radicalization would take hold and Cleveland Sellers Jr. would rise in the ranks and, then, in the flash of one horrific night, fall.

8 BLACK POWER

AMONG MARTIN LUTHER KING'S most famous phrases is one that revealed his profound understanding of the way history works, of the time it takes for change to manifest. "The arc of the moral universe is long, but it bends toward justice," he said. He knew he would not live to see the country fully abandon its racism, nor would he have the chance to celebrate the redemption of the South and its legacy of oppression. But he comprehended instinctively that beneficial change was inexorable, that politics was progressive by definition (despite sometimes forceful resistance), so he could envision a future when skin color no longer defined a person.

The freedom movement also included prominent public fig- ures whose universes bent in other directions, whose imaginations presented distinctions of race, class and culture, whose hopes were not placed in a utopian vision of social cooperation. The arc of that moral universe led to a nationalistic interpretation of the future, one that reinforced a separate-but-equal socio-economic construct. Until the end of his life, when his views began to widen profoundly, Malcolm X described a plain racial dichotomy and preached black self-sufficiency. The white man, he said, would *never* allow the black man to be free; the Negro would have to overcome his inferiority complex and learn to fend for himself. SNCC leaders in the mid-1960s began to put Malcolm's lessons into practice, adopting a similar view of the "honky" and glorifying African history and culture. This shift within SNCC arguably placed it on a path to nowhere, but for a while that path was well-paved and well-trod. And surely the ideas that fueled the pilgrimage found their way into the wider society, especially academia—so all was by no means lost.

BY THE SUMMER OF 1965, SNCC had a fleet of 30 vehicles, about 200 paid staffers, 250 full-time volunteers, fundraising programs and an annual budget of about $800,000. The Selma-Montgomery March had galvanized activists in Alabama and focused attention on Lowndes County. Sellers, now based in Atlanta, spent much of his time on the road checking in with SNCC's various projects and seeking to forge coalitions with other civil and labor rights organizations, anti-war groups and independence movements. He visited with Cesar Chavez in California to learn about Mexican grape pickers. He endorsed the Puerto Rican call for autonomy. He sought ways to oppose the Vietnam War. "The movement was shifting from a focus on civil rights to human rights," he said.

Jim Forman arranged the purchase of a two-story downtown office building in Atlanta with the objective of installing a large printing press. To do so, the staff walled up the garage. Now SNCC could publish newsletters, pamphlets and more. The research office was staffed with four or five people who followed media stories, sought information about legal matters and helped SNCC leaders with planning. The office included a photography department and a finance department. It was a robust operation, a solid home base. Sellers now wielded real influence. Despite much strategic and tactical uncertainty, he was glad to have the opportunity to help determine the organization's direction and optimistic that better management would enable SNCC to achieve many of its ambitious goals. "You don't always know how your seed is going to grow, but if the weather doesn't kill it, there's a chance it will grow at a most opportune time," he said. He would remain part of the top leadership, SNCC's number three man, through 1966 and much of 1967.

Meanwhile, Carmichael was in charge of the Lowndes County project in Alabama and accumulating more leadership bona fides. He was making allies among black farmers, many of whom were armed and unwilling to embrace King's nonviolent philosophy. Carmichael and his Alabama colleagues, such as Bill Hansen and Fay Bellamy, had made inroads but they hadn't succeeded in getting many blacks registered to vote. That was about to change. The effort to set up the Lowndes County Freedom Organization, a political party not unlike the MFDP and a precursor to the Black Panther Party, was triggered by a chance discovery: SNCC Research Director Jack Minnis had found an obscure law on the Alabama books that permitted the formation of county-based independent parties. When Carmichael was told about it, he immediately saw an opportunity to shift from Mississippi to something new in the state next door. The population of Lowndes County, situated between Selma and Montgomery and extending about 35 miles southward, was 15,000, of which 12,000 were black—and none of the black residents were registered to vote. It took only a year for Carmichael to get the county's blacks, already excited by the recent Selma-Montgomery March, completely organized behind an assurgent political effort. Enthusiasm mostly ran high, though some were concerned that forming an all-black party was only a means to sustain segregation, while others, conditioned by centuries of oppression and bigotry, felt inadequate to the task. Nevertheless, the Lowndes County Voters League was established, and it adopted a black panther, suggested by Dorothy Zellner, as its ballot symbol. Back at SNCC headquarters, Sellers was providing his friend with essential funding and staffing support.

That year SNCC was beset with problems—organizational, philosophical, political and emotional. The integrationist-enfranchisement phase of the freedom movement was over, more or less, with just one more large-scale protest on the horizon, the March Against Fear, and that was almost accidental. The focus of freedom movement participants was turning increasingly outward. They perceived themselves as pawns in a geopolitical game; they connected domestic oppression with political and economic phenomena outside the U.S. They questioned why blacks and other Americans who had been systematically marginalized should be expected to "defend democracy" in faraway places like Vietnam. They began to see themselves in solidarity with other oppressed groups and victims of Western influence and aggression: the people of Southeast Asia, the people of Palestine, the people of Puerto Rico and Central America and especially the people of Africa who were struggling to rid themselves of the legacy of European colonialism. This growing internationalism and pan-Africanism was not entirely new; activists had been acutely aware of economic and class divides, both domestic and international, for years. One could argue that a form of black nationalism was first articulated coherently by Booker T. Washington during the second part of the 19th century when he worked to establish black schools, and by

W.E.B. Du Bois, who advocated not only equal education opportunities but full civic enfranchisement.

Scholars such as Peniel Joseph, author of *Dark Days, Bright Nights*, and Robert Chase, a former public historian at the Avery Research Center for African American History and Culture in Charleston, South Carolina, now at Stony Brook University, argue that Black Power was essentially synonymous with the black freedom movement, that it provided the underlying foundation upon which activists pursued their various goals over the decades and that what is commonly known as the civil rights movement of 1956-1965 was really only a nonviolent phase in a much broader effort. When Stokely Carmichael, sick and tired of being jailed repeatedly on trumped up charges, cried "Black Power!" during the 1966 March Against Fear in support of James Meredith, he was not signaling a strategic departure; he was announcing a return to the fundamental ideas that had energized the freedom movement since Reconstruction. Indeed, he wasn't the first to utter that phrase or articulate it's precepts. Adam Clayton Powell, who represented Harlem in the U.S. House, used it a month before the Meredith March in a speech at Howard University and referred to a version of Black Power in earlier writings. Novelist Richard Wright published a book in 1954 titled "Black Power," referring to Africa's anti-colonial efforts. North Carolina NAACP leader Robert Williams spoke of the principles of Black Power of during the 1950s.

The Nation of Islam, founded in 1930, was a separatist movement informed by the teachings of Marcus Garvey that beseeched blacks to wake up and unshackle themselves from the influence and corruption of the "white devils." What Garvey, Powell, Malcolm X, Carmichael and former President Barack Obama each have said, in their own way, is: "We have to have a political voice of our own"—disenfranchised black people certainly, but also others with no one who genuinely represents their interests in the halls

of power, Chase said. This is what's meant by "Black Power," and
recent scholarship has broadened its definition and better revealed
its far-reaching impact. "Black Power remains the most misunder-
stood social movement of the postwar era," wrote Joseph. "It was
demonized as the civil rights movement's 'evil twin' and stereo-
typed as a politics of rage practiced by gun-toting Black Panthers.
Because of this, the movement's supple intellectual provocations,
pragmatic local character, and domestic- and foreign-policy cri-
tiques remain on the fringes of America's memory of the 1960s."

Black Power found its most nuanced expression at the neighborhood level, Joseph wrote, where revolutionary rhetoric
blended with political pragmatism. Malcolm X is a prime example.
In Nation of Islam mosques and in the streets of black neighborhoods, Malcolm X usually glorified Elijah Muhammad, vilified
the white oppressors and admonished complacent blacks to stand
up and claim what was rightfully theirs. But merely parroting the
party line was impossible for Malcolm; he was too smart for that.
Questions and doubts began to seep into his thinking, and by the
early 1960s, he was eager to engage with other civil rights activists
and he struggled to reconcile (unsuccessfully) his loyalty to the
Nation with his interest in authentic Islam and pragmatic political
solutions, according to Manning Marable's important biography,
"Malcolm X: A Life of Reinvention."

The Black Power movement, which reached maturity in the
late 1960s, had a strong Southern component, noted Chase, refer-
encing Carmichael's 1965-66 campaign for political enfranchisement in Mississippi and Alabama. Carmichael's work led to the
formation of the Lowndes County Freedom Organization, which
would become the Black Panther Party. Up north, Malcolm X was
arguing that urban blacks needed to shed the mental shackles of
slavery and believe in themselves and their rights. The logic was
simple: For African Americans to share power, they had to form

black-led organizations that could challenge white hegemony. Sellers was fully on board with this idea and helped make SNCC an organization with a broader view of the world, even as he coped with less philosophical matters such as fundraising, which was becoming increasingly difficult, opposition to established political parties (especially the Democratic Party) and a growing sense of isolation. SNCC was changing, partly due to an internal push-pull confusion over identity, mission and strategic agenda, and partly because of external forces. As the group grew in size and influence, divisions within became visible and debates multiplied, especially concerning what roles members should play, what purpose should be served and what sort of administration was needed. "By 1965, SNCC had become, in the eyes of supporters and critics, not simply a civil rights organization but a part of the New Left: an amorphous body of young activists seeking new ideological alternatives to conventional liberalism," wrote Clayborne Carson in *In Struggle*. In 1965, SNCC included many whites, and this caused many to wonder whether it was being co-opted, how it could effectively pursue its agenda and who exactly was in charge. Sellers was torn. He believed in the concept of the Beloved Community, in which blacks and whites found common ground, but he knew that to get there likely would require each to walk along a separate path, at least for a while. Sellers' definition of Black Power was not the militant one portrayed by the media, but it did encompass the notion of black self-determination, and that in turn led SNCC to a racial fork in the road. Whites in the organization were allies and friends, and that wouldn't change, but perhaps they could best help the cause by organizing in poor white communities. First things first. You can't include whites in a Beloved Community if they refuse to embrace blacks as equals.

* ❀ *

THE DISAPPOINTMENT OF the Atlantic City convention forced many, white and black, to reject institutional cooperation in favor of a more radical approach. Predominantly white liberal groups, such as Students for a Democratic Society, and influential white activists such as Howard Zinn (who wrote a sympathetic portrait of a still youthful SNCC, published in 1964, called *SNCC: The New Abolitionists*), were seeking alliances with SNCC or were eager to portray the group as part of a larger, national effort to address global injustice. Various ideas—derived from Marxist theory, anti-colonial literature, liberal economics and revolutionary accounts from Africa and Asia—were discussed openly and influenced many of SNCC's members. Concern for the plight of people outside the U.S. was increasingly evident. In particular, the war in Vietnam was galvanizing protesters from a variety of groups, including SNCC. In March 1965, the U.S. military initiated Operation Flaming Dart, Operation Rolling Thunder and Operation Arc Light, intense bombing campaigns in North Vietnam that escalated the war dramatically. Already, Jim Forman and Bob Moses had publicly criticized U.S. military involvement in Southeast Asia, citing the war as an example of American hypocrisy. The government would go to great lengths and expense to protect freedom abroad but do to little for its own people.

At the same time, serious tensions were developing inside the organization between emergent factions, Sellers recalled. "The most flamboyant faction was composed of a group of 'stars,' who at various times were referred to as 'philosophers, existentialists, anarchists, floaters and freedom-high niggers,'" he wrote in his memoir. "Most of them were well educated. And they were about evenly divided between whites and blacks. They were integrationists who strongly believed that every individual had the right and responsibility to follow the dictates of his conscience, no matter what.... My characterization of the Freedom-High position probably reveals my bias. I was one of their staunchest opponents. I considered them impractical. SNCC was not a debating society. It was an action organization." Floaters were those, both black and white, who held integrationist views and were adept at long philosophical debates about the nature of oppression, the influences of childhood, the forms of revolution and the way political identity is forged in the crucible of the struggle. They were remnants of SNCC's early phase. Hardliners like Sellers were black, mostly nationalistic and more eager to act than to talk. They were representative of SNCC's new direction. They weren't anti-white, Sellers said. In fact, they resented the portrayal of Black Power advocates as radical militants who refused to collaborate with whites. The seeds of this false argument, posed by many in the media and by those who feared the nationalist strain now seeping into the movement, were planted in Atlantic City, when backers of the Mississippi Freedom Democratic Party broke with traditional Democrats. And the seeds were watered soon after in Alabama with the emergence of the Lowndes County Freedom Organization. Some of the hyperbole of Black Power surely instilled concern, even fear, in certain observers, and some activists exploited Black Power in an effort to provoke disgruntled people to take actions that were not always well thought out. "But hyperbole is important to get black people to buy into it," Sellers said. "No one wanted to burn cities down. That's wasted energy. People's response comes out of their pain and suffering. It's not always perfect."

9   IN CHARGE

IN NOVEMBER 1965, SNCC held its annual election upon shifting sands. Floaters and hardliners agreed that field operators ought to be unburdened by the organization's thickening bureaucracy, and some were grumbling about John Lewis' leadership as chairman. Hadn't his stubbornness about Selma caused unnecessary conflict and expenditures? A change was necessary, they thought. A restructuring resulted in the formation of a large executive committee and a Secretariat consisting of chairman, executive secretary and a new position, program secretary. The Secretariat would be responsible for making day-to-day decisions; the 20-member executive committee would represent the interests of the full range of members, from radical pacifist to radical militant. Despite the grumbling, Lewis was re-elected chairman and Forman was re-elected executive secretary. To his surprise, the 21-year-old Cleveland Sellers was elected program secretary. He spent the next few months cleaning house—imposing rules on the use of the automobile inventory, asserting revised definitions of SNCC membership and advancing a more consistent political agenda. He ran into trouble, of course. Many resisted what they considered an overly bureaucratic approach. Many argued that decentralization and regional autonomy were what distinguished SNCC in the first place and should not be compromised.

By this time, Sellers noted, SNCC was a substantial operation with a large staff and big funding goals it struggled to achieve. "You had people who started out with the idea that you needed to stay small and you needed to stay out of that bureaucratic kind of thing. But you ended up having the kinds of tentacles that required you have some kind of bureaucracy there in order for you to manage those things," Sellers said. It was a challenge. The Black Power and anti-war movements were heating up; events in the American South and urban North demanded attention. Sellers occupied the hot seat. "During that period, with Black Power and the anti-war movement and all those kinds of things, I played a very intricate role as the program director of SNCC. And my first task was to get the others, the chairman and the executive director, on board with what I was trying to do, so that we would all be in concert." Sellers had the right personality for this kind of work. The stress was mostly internalized. He remained outwardly quiet, calm, laid back. "But I had a pretty good operation, a pretty good office, a pretty good staff and we just kept moving the organization forward."

Even Carmichael resisted his friend's management style. The two men battled fiercely, with Carmichael accusing Sellers of becoming a bureaucrat more concerned about cars than people and programs, and Sellers defending himself: "I'm saying, I have a hundred people out here. I need to have them in places where there's work going on and that they are there to do that kind of work. I can't have them in Mexico, you know for the siesta that lasts for six months, with an automobile that belong to us, that has insurance on it that ain't no good in Mexico." *Somebody* had to oversee these logistical and administrative priorities, he said. "And I think he appreciated that when he went to Lowndes County. And then he's calling me to ask me, 'I need a couple of organizers down here.' Well, okay. We're gonna work that out for you. We're gonna try to take care of that. 'I need a vehicle.' Okay. We're gonna try to get you a vehicle. But see, we have to find where those vehicles are."

It was a challenge to balance logistical and financial matters with the changing focus and strategy of the organization, now concerned with the Vietnam War, urban rebellions, examples of neo-colonialism in the world and other problems viewed as interconnected with the freedom movement in the U.S. "How do you corral that energy and make it productive?" Sellers asked. "We had a lot to grapple with at that particular time."

Discord within the organization flared especially brightly during the 1966 Atlanta Project, a special SNCC initiative directed by Bill Ware. Aware that many blacks in urban neighborhoods were feeling excluded from the civil rights movement, Ware and other organizers had launched a grassroots outreach effort in the southern capital to organize young blacks in the city, getting them to push for equal rights, demand better of Atlanta's political leadership and support Julian Bond's campaign for Congress.

But black militants had "infiltrated" the program, Sellers said, and had begun emphasizing the politics of racial identity. Ware and other leaders of the more radical Atlanta Project advocated racial separatism rather than nonviolence and cross-cultural cooperation.

What's more, the small Atlanta Project staff, ensconced in the desperately poor Vine City neighborhood, was operating as if it were an autonomous organization. It stopped responding to Sellers, Carmichael, Forman, Bellamy and others in the main office only about a mile away. This was a problem: SNCC had hoped to put Black Power concepts to practical use, much the way rebel forces in other parts of the world also provided social services.

Many of the Atlanta separatists were from the urban North, and many had joined SNCC just as the organization was shifting its focus to political and economic objectives, that is, Black Power. Before long, SNCC's leadership team had a complicated mutiny on their hands. A $3,000 contribution meant to help SNCC build support for Bond's embattled campaign was appropriated by the Atlanta group. At the March staff meeting, the Atlanta Project team presented a position paper presenting arguments for fostering a new black consciousness, removing whites from the organization and rejecting the more pragmatic and conciliatory views still held by many in SNCC. "The major thesis of the position paper was 'that the form of white participation, as practiced in the past, is now obsolete,'" wrote Clayborne Carson, director of the Martin Luther King Papers Project. "On a pragmatic level, the authors asserted that many blacks were 'intimidated by the presence of whites, because of their knowledge of the power that whites have over their lives.' A single white person who participated in a meeting of black people could change the tone of that meeting: 'People would immediately start talking about 'brotherhood,' 'love,' etc.; race would not be discussed.' A climate had to be created, they argued, in which black people could freely express themselves. SNCC, they wrote, had isolated itself from blacks because of the presence of whites." Whites were not capable of understanding the black experience, yet they exercised influence on policy, the Atlanta Project staff argued. And SNCC, by continuing to include whites, had alienated blacks and reduced its ability to galvanize them.

These ideas were not entirely new—the role of whites had been hotly debated for years—but with the rise of Black Power, the forceful legacy of Malcolm X and the tactical changes underway through the freedom movement, they gained currency. When the Atlanta position paper found its way to the national media and was presented as if it were official SNCC policy, it compromised the organization, Sellers said. "That document was never voted on in SNCC at all. It was never an official document.... We didn't take the time to clarify and distinguish between the Atlanta Project position and our position. But our position was never to hurt or to harm any person who had contributed." Rather, SNCC leaders were exploring ways to "move on," to get to "the next level," to absorb new lessons and develop new strategies that rejected no one. "We're talking about empowering this community, self-determination. How do you begin to resurrect those values, and how do you begin to build community so that when it is beginning to go into this coalition, this big coalition, it will be able to maintain its identity and its understanding of what the goals and objectives are? So you bring those groups together and you maintain that kind of thing."

The SNCC leadership, including Carmichael and Sellers, openly rejected the arguments made by the Atlanta separatists in the interest of keeping SNCC together. Nevertheless, the appeal of Black Power was strong, and Carmichael soon would find himself in a position to promote this more radical agenda. In May 1966, after three years as chairman of SNCC, Lewis was re-elected at the group's meeting near Nashville. But Carmichael, sensing an opportunity, challenged him, and the next morning Lewis was de-elected. Lewis wasn't black enough, wasn't militant enough, Carmichael and others had argued. Sellers quietly agreed.

The organization claimed it "needed someone who could stand up to Martin Luther King and Lyndon Johnson," said Lewis, today a Congressman from Georgia. But King didn't need more challengers; there were enough of those. He needed help. "He was like my big brother," Lewis said. "We truly believed in the idea of a truly multiracial democracy."

Carmichael believed in Black Power and all it represented, and he was ready to assume the top leadership role. A few days later, Lewis was gone. He had seen the writing on the wall. Sellers was caught in the middle. He was no pacifist. Like most SNCC members, he was ready to defend himself (and others) if lives were threatened. He was a believer in nonviolent resistance as a tactic, not a way of life. Nonviolence, taking the high road, was the only moral way to influence the Powers-That-Be. But he was no militant extremist either. He perceived the nationalistic, exclusionary ideology of the Black Power movement as a "necessary phase" enabling blacks to mine their history and define their identity. Empowerment of blacks depended in part on identity politics, Sellers said. Black Power wasn't a bad thing, it wasn't about violent confrontation, it was an affirmation. First, blacks had to acknowledge their own culture before they could hope to reconcile it with society at large. "A period of confrontation inevitably would lead to a period of engagement," he said. "Eventually, political and economic issues had to be addressed, not [only] moral issues." Sellers believed then that all of society needed improving, and that all of society was required in the effort, even if some of the work would demand that black people look after their own interests. "If the principle is justice, how can we embrace violence? Civil rights is about building community."

The desire to build community: that was another outcome of the May staff meeting, a growing consensus that SNCC ought to focus on energizing people at the grassroots level and promote black consciousness. In early June, Sellers, Carmichael and Stanley Wise were in Little Rock, Arkansas, checking in on SNCC colleagues, drumming up support and mobilizing residents when James Meredith, who had desegregated the University of Mississippi four years earlier, chose to walk 200 miles from Memphis to Jackson as a public demonstration to encourage blacks to vote now that the Voting Rights Act was law. His March Against Fear was interrupted, however, when a 41-year-old white Memphis man named Aubrey James Norvell ambushed Meredith on the Mississippi side of the border and fired three shotgun blasts, injuring the activist in the back and legs. Meredith was transported to a Memphis hospital and soon recovered enough to continue the march. Quickly, many others decided to join the effort. The SNCC leaders drove the short distance to Memphis to show their support. Civil rights leaders were converging on the scene, including Martin Luther King and CORE leader Floyd McKissick.

Sellers and the other SNCC members strongly encouraged Meredith to resume his march, and the idea was embraced with fervor by participating civil rights organizations such as SCLC, CORE, MFDP and the Medical Committee for Human Rights. The armed Deacons of Defense and Justice from Louisiana arrived to provide protection along the periphery (something to which the nonviolent King did not object). Carmichael convinced a reluctant SNCC executive committee to support the effort, though many in the organization were wary of marches since the Selma turmoil the year before. Carmichael told them the march could be used to help organize local residents in Mississippi's Second Congressional District, an argument that succeeded in tipping the scales in favor of direct action. This wouldn't just be another march; this would be a chance to register people to vote, to talk about education reform and economic development and community building. During rallies around the time of the Meredith

March, the phrase "black power for black people," shortened to "Black Power," and other combinations of these two loaded words were used liberally, by Carmichael, Willie Ricks and many others. The general concept of black empowerment was old; the label "black," however, was replacing "negro" and "colored," signaling a new self-awareness and an attempt to move past the semantics of the Jim Crow era. Bob Smith, Ricks and Sellers added fuel to the flames, distributing leaflets and placards to rally participants in Greenwood, a halfway point on the route. Local police were deployed in the city and resorted to the use of tear gas, but that did nothing to dampen the enthusiasm of the crowds. Many knew, or at least recognized, Carmichael, who had been stationed in Greenwood during Freedom Summer two years earlier. On June 16, Carmichael was arrested for trespassing on public property as he tried to camp for the night, resulting in an afternoon spent behind bars. He emerged from jail angry and tired, rejoining the protesters who had by nightfall gathered in a park. There he gave his famous speech, declaring, "This is the 27th time I have been arrested and I ain't going to jail no more! The only way we gonna stop them white men from whuppin' us is to take over. What we gonna start sayin' now is Black Power!"

That improvised speech changed everything. It fired up local blacks, propelled Carmichael onto a national stage and provided a still somewhat floundering SNCC with an ideological focus. It also worried SCLC leaders who pleaded with King to condemn this new battle cry and all it implied and to repudiate its proponents. King did take some distance from the Black Power concept, but he refused to break with SNCC and its leaders. Days marching together helped forge strong bonds between him and the SNCC activists. Sellers developed a profound fondness for King and a deep admiration for his riveting nightly speeches and humble demeanor. "Though he was forced by political circumstance to disavow Black Power for himself and for his organization, there has never been any question in my mind since our March Against Fear that Dr. King was a staunch ally and true brother," Sellers wrote in his memoir.

Sellers was asked to go to Jackson to make preparations for the final rally. Some on the SNCC team were sidelined by SCLC people trying to mitigate the impact of the Black Power cry. Despite the political wrangling, the march ended strongly, with about 15,000 entering Jackson on June 26, making this the largest civil rights event in Mississippi's history. All along the way, activists registered local residents to vote. Sellers was energized. "From SNCC's point of view, the march was a huge success."

10 REFUSING THE DRAFT

SNCC IN 1966 needed a lot of work behind the scenes, even as its public face was changing dramatically, becoming more verbose, radical, challenging. Inside, memoranda and position papers were being written to reflect shifting attitudes and ideas and to express solidarity with freedom movements elsewhere in the world. The big picture was now in view through a windshield cleared of its domestic grit. As chairman, Stokely Carmichael refined his Black Power script and became much in demand as a public speaker. He was often on the road, leaving charge of the operation to Sellers and Ruby Doris in Atlanta. "In fact, even the time I could spend in Atlanta working with Cleve and Ruby Doris on the day-to-day running of the organization was much less than I'd expected and wanted," Carmichael wrote in his memoir. "So these burdens fell heavy on Cleve, Ruby Doris, and the executive committee at a time when there would be some heavy internal challenges to face. I wasn't at all comfortable with that, but it really couldn't be helped."

Nevertheless, there were many opportunities for Sellers to join the front lines of the movement outside of Atlanta. He traveled regularly to check on SNCC's various projects and to meet with student and labor activists elsewhere to share information and forge alliances, informal and formal. He also accompanied Carmichael on his speech circuit both as a de facto manager and unofficial security officer. It was not unusual during this period for Sellers, Carmichael and other prominent SNCC leaders to carry guns for protection when travelling by car, Sellers said. Carmichael's stage rhetoric was forceful—divisive, many observers complained. The Meredith March had ended with a massive rally at the state capitol where he exhorted the marchers and their supporters in Jackson to "build a power base ... so strong that we will bring [whites] to their knees every time they mess with us."

The sentiment was understandable, and it excited many activists, but it did not garner the support of the majority of blacks who preferred the moderate, integrationist approach advanced by King and others. This was partly a result of media coverage. Black Power advocates such as Carmichael, Malcolm X, Rap Brown, Bobby Seale and others advocating a nationalistic and militant agenda, were viewed as fringe radicals by most blacks and as dangerous subversives by government and the press. Addressing a national gathering of newspaper editors in 1967, Floyd McKissick of CORE complained that their stories were sensationalistic and avoided describing the legitimate concerns of those seeking self-determination. "All you can see, all you can hear, are two words: 'Black Power,'" he told them. "You would like us to stand in the streets and chant

'Black Power' for your amusement." News organizations were not particularly interested in writing about the actual condition of black America; they preferred loud stories that vilified extremism and faulted anyone for failing to abide by accepted social rules.

Civil rights groups saw a significant ramping up of covert infiltration and heightened scrutiny by the FBI and other government agencies. Carmichael—and by extension Sellers and others—were high on the list of subversives under surveillance. Those months, from mid-1966 through 1967, were a period of living dangerously for SNCC. Its new emphasis on black consciousness was crystallizing, but it was not winning over average black citizens wholesale. Instead, it seemed to offer SNCC's enemies an opportunity to foster division within the freedom movement and animosity between black leaders and government authorities. An irony of the second half of the 1960s is that the enfranchisement promised by the Civil Rights Act of 1964 and Voting Rights Act of 1965 turned into a bitter street fight that further radicalized many activists. But to what end? Self-determination and black consciousness might have been the goals, but unless the political system made room for such autonomy (or was forced to make room for it), it could not be realized. Was the goal a nation within a nation? Was it some sort of reunion with sub-Saharan Africa? Or was it a form of power sharing? And if so, why advocate separatism? These dilemmas echoed within SNCC and CORE and the Black Panthers and other black nationalist groups during this phase of the freedom struggle, never to be fully resolved.

This is not to say that nothing was achieved. The Black Power movement led to an artistic and cultural flowering, much of which was appreciated by people around the world. Black studies programs at colleges provided a formal structure for the inculcation of black history and culture. Some black intellectuals, such as Carmichael, looked to Africa for the answer. Others—Nikki Giovanni, Amiri

Baraka, Nina Simone, Vertamae Smart-Grosvenor—turned to the arts to develop an invigorated black identity. Many more were left out, unable to pursue a college education or join an intellectual or political movement. City dwellers, deprived of a voice for so long, took to the streets in frustration.

ALL OF THIS was carefully monitored by the FBI, which was obsessed at the time with the Red Menace and anti-government agitation. The agency opened its file on Sellers with a January 16, 1967 dispatch from Chicago that alerted Illinois officials in the U.S. Attorney's office and Secret Service of Sellers' and Carmichael's travel itinerary. The two men were leaving Chicago for Philadelphia and Washington, D.C., after which their paths would diverge. Carmichael would continue on to New York City and Detroit before returning to Chicago; Sellers would proceed to Baltimore, New York City, Detroit, then San Francisco. During this period, SNCC was actively exploring ways to extend its reach to the urban North and organize residents of the big cities facing institutional forms of economic and social discrimination. Sellers also was interested in learning from others and forging alliances. Perhaps this would help strengthen SNCC at a time when its political posturing and Black Power ideology, exaggerated in the media, was rubbing many the wrong way. In part, the organization was trying to counteract a corrosion of support it was experiencing in the South as a result of its perceived militancy. SNCC leaders were acutely aware of the government's surveillance and propaganda campaign, and they hoped that by winning both ideological and financial backers around the country they could bolster their efforts and agenda. But the government was looking for ways to stop SNCC altogether. The short FBI memo, entitled "Racial Matters," included flight information and other details. An agent boarded the plane in Chicago and reported that "Carmichael was dressed in blue levis [sic], a blue overall coat, grey topcoat and wearing sunglasses. Sellers had on a black fur cap and was wearing a grey overcoat."

The FBI grew increasingly concerned about Sellers in the following months, closely tracking his movements, warning the State Department's Passport Division of planned international travel, and gathering background information. A July 31 FBI secret report noted that Sellers was issued a passport [in New York City] on July 17, 1967, passport number H-754994. "The passport was valid for three years for travel to all countries except Cuba, Mainland China, North Korea and North Vietnam....According to the record, Sellers was to depart 'by organized tour' on July 18, 1967, to go to the Union of Soviet Socialist Republics for one month....[He] advised that he had never been married and that in the event of death or accident he requested that his mother, Pauline T. Sellers, 633 Fredrick Avenue Denmark, South Carolina, be notified."

But he didn't go. His file shows that he put the passport in a suitcase that was accidentally transported to Zambia. "I have been unable to get in contact with the party that has the suitcase," Sellers informed officials. "When I get the passport, I will bring it in for cancellation." In fact, Sellers rarely left the country; most of his travels, closely tracked by the government, were domestic. Throughout 1967 he visited Chicago; Tougaloo and Jackson, Mississippi; Daytona Beach, Florida; Baton Rouge, Louisiana; Roxbury, Massachusetts; and Honolulu, according to the FBI. In mid-August he made a trip to Japan, representing SNCC, to attend a memorial program honoring the victims of the nuclear disasters in Nagasaki and Hiroshima. On his way back to the States, he stopped in Oakland to meet with the Black Panthers and learn about their social outreach programs and observe the party's food drives, Sellers said.

Sellers' thick FBI file strongly hints at the concern officials harbored about the activist's associations and political ideology. Either they worried that he was a dangerous leftist radical, or they wished to portray him as such in an effort to demonize him and marginalize SNCC. The file takes note of an article appearing in The State newspaper of Columbia, South Carolina, on February 10, 1968, that reviewed Sellers' various arrests during the previous three years: in Cambridge, Maryland, in May 1964 while demonstrating against former Alabama governor George Wallace; in March 1966 in Washington, D.C., during an apartheid protest with James Forman, John Lewis, Willie Ricks and Bill Hall; in April 1966, in Jackson, Mississippi, for trespassing and disturbing the peace and in September 1966 in Atlanta for "distributing insurrectionary material."

"The article states that Sellers took part in the Nashville, Tennessee, riot last April, but he was not arrested," the FBI report states. "The Congressional Committee said it had no record that Sellers had traveled to either Havana, Cuba, or Hanoi, North Vietnam, although there have been reports he has made such trips."

Sellers surely was at his most radical in 1967, the year he refused induction into the military, the year he tried to align SNCC with international revolutionary trends. On July 27, 1967, police stopped Sellers and two others along a highway in Baton Rouge, Louisiana, and arrested them when a gun was found in the car. They had accompanied Carmichael, who was instructing students on the campus of Southern University "to develop a concept of peoplehood." Sellers and his two colleagues told police they were Carmichael's bodyguards and that the gun belonged to their colleague. They were briefly held until Carmichael spoke with the police and promised that he would leave the state immediately.

Sellers' close association with Carmichael evidently prompted much of the early scrutiny. An August 29, 1967, memorandum from "SAC, Atlanta" (Special Agent in Charge) to "Director, FBI" included evidence of inside informants who had infiltrated SNCC.

It will be recalled that in May, 1967, SELLERS was replaced as Program Director of SNCC by RALPH FEATHERSTONE.

On 7/24/67 [redacted] advised that although SELLERS does not hold an elected position in SNCC at this time, he is "a dedicated person to STOKELY CARMICHAEL."

On 8/28/67, this same source advised that SELLERS has returned to the United States after a trip to Japan. He has not yet arrived in Atlanta, but when he does come he will reside at [redacted].

SELLERS' activities will be investigated in accordance with instructions contained in referenced Bureau airtel to Albany, 8/21/67.

IT WAS A VERY BUSY TIME. Carmichael and Sellers simultaneously strived to run SNCC (adjusting its emphasis and programming), engage in various activities across the country and abroad, devise a set of positions on matters ranging from African revolutions to the ways blacks in America can leverage capitalism to the war in Southeast Asia. Nothing seemed to escape SNCC's attention: labor disputes were noted, campus complaints registered, court cases examined. SNCC published statements on most of these matters.

As the Vietnam War heated up, Sellers was among the first to put into practice SNCC's recommendations for opposing it: he refused to join the Army. On February 6, 1967, Sellers wrote a biting letter to Mrs. N.P. Smook at the post office in Bamberg, South Carolina:

Dear Madame:

It seems to me that you racists take pride in trying to induct me because of my affiliation with Stokely Carmichael and the Student

*Nonviolent Coordinating Committee. I would like to inform you
that I am proud of all my affiliations and thanks to them I can really
understand who my real enemy is. It is not the Viet Con [sic] but you
dumb white racists.*

His letter was sent to the post office because that is where one
went to register for the draft in those days. Sellers went on to defend
his right to avoid the draft on medical grounds ("a heart defect")
and because of pending court cases, including one in Mississippi
that "stems from supposedly assaulting a white racist, like yourself, a policeman." Two months later, a more famous black activist,
25-year-old Muhammad Ali, refused induction into the U.S. Army
for all the same reasons, attracted much media attention and triggered much debate around dinner tables across America.

On February 24 that year, Sellers filed a civil action against Defense
Secretary Robert McNamara, Gov. Lester Maddox of Georgia,
Gov. Robert E. McNair of South Carolina and the Selective Service,
arguing that the Universal Military Training and Service Act—the
draft—was unconstitutional. He asked that a permanent injunction be granted by the court to prevent the draft boards in Georgia
and South Carolina from inducting him and any other black man
into the armed forces on grounds that blacks were systematically
excluded from Selective Service boards in those two states.

Sellers' suit alleged that he had been drafted based on race and
political affiliation, that draft boards were illegal because they
were not representative and that the draft deprived him of his
constitutional right to due process. But his complaints, argued by
prominent black attorney Howard Moore Jr., were dismissed by
the court. Sellers soon would face a jury trial, then find himself
imprisoned for four long months.

11   UNDER FIRE

AN IRONY OF the 1967-68 period was that SNCC and other black organizations were widely perceived by the American public as insular, even racist, emphasizing militant nationalism, even as these same organizations were in fact forging new alliances and discovering much in common with other groups seeking liberty and justice. It was really an alignment of the left. The SNCC leadership was part of a coalition that included Cesar Chavez and others in the labor movement, Native Americans who were now holding the banner of "Red Power," representatives of the Puerto Rican independence movement, anti-apartheid fighters and anti-imperialistic voices critical of U.S. influence in Central and South America. Politically engaged black people in the U.S. increasingly were viewing themselves not as uniquely crippled by the legacy of slavery but as part of a larger effort to resist capitalistic and imperialistic oppression. Blacks were not only part of this global movement, they were leaders of this global movement, setting an example for others and, at some level, making them aware of it. "You have to have what everybody else has, and that is some knowledge and history about who you are," Sellers said. "And you have to debunk the whole notion that African Americans grew up in the cotton field." Blacks were as capable of sophisticated political thinking and effective social action as anyone else.

This complex, fast-evolving period, with its expansive implications for history, impacted Sellers in other, more personal ways. It surely played a part in his turbulent relationship with Helen Saundra "Sandy" Duncan. Sandy was a young woman immersed in the movement when she joined Sellers and organizer James Harris during lunch one day in 1966 in Jackson, Mississippi, just ahead of the final rally of the Meredith March. Sellers was SNCC's 21-year-old program director at the time and under terrific pressure from various quarters. Sandy Duncan was pretty, smart and well-spoken; he took an interest in the 18-year-old, and after the march, he invited her to live with him in Atlanta. She already knew some members of SNCC and soon met others. She got involved in the work even as she pursued her own interests, such as photography.

The romantic relationship sprouted during a hectic period when Sellers was overseeing SNCC's wide-ranging operations and keeping a close eye on Carmichael, who was in demand as a speaker, travelling widely and making trouble for SNCC with his freestyle approach and militant rhetoric. "I was the only one who could reign in Stokely, and clean up the mess afterwards," Sellers recalled. He did so willingly, though not without a degree of exasperation. The young administrator worked long hours, much of the time coping with fallout from the Black Power ideology the organization had embraced. Attacks came from every direction. After a heady first few weeks with Sandy, the pressures and demands of SNCC recaptured Sellers' attention. He had less time for her, and she began to feel abandoned and alone.

Matters only intensified: A minor riot in Atlanta in response to a white police officer's lethal shooting of a black man resulted in the arrest of Carmichael on the following day, even though the Black Power spokesman wasn't on the scene. City officials and the news media blamed SNCC "demagogues" for the unrest, not the police officer. The episode and its aftermath kept Sellers busy at the office—and away from Sandy. In late September 1967, after returning from a two-day trip representing SNCC, Sellers discovered that Sandy was having an affair with Rap Brown. He complained, explaining that she and Brown were threatening the unity of SNCC. Sandy was contrite but confused, and she agreed to end her affair with Brown. The next month, Sellers and Sandy relocated to Orangeburg. He wanted some distance from SNCC's daily grind; he also was considering enrolling in college and he wanted to work with students on black empowerment initiatives. "I decided that I had pretty much been around SNCC enough," he said. "It was time to transition, and I was thinking I was going back to college like a number of other people had already done."

By that time, he had given up his title as program director. In the spring of 1967 he had opted not to run again for the office, and in May, Ralph Featherstone had assumed Sellers' former post. Carmichael, too, had opted not to seek re-election, preferring to return to roll-up-your-sleeves grassroots organizing. Sellers had been growing increasingly ambivalent in 1967 about his role in SNCC, but he had not fully relinquished his commitment and responsibilities. He was especially interested in SNCC's outreach to college students. The organization, though shrinking for lack of funding, now had a "campus coordinator" among its staff and set goals to recruit young supporters, institute new programs, and raise money.

NOW BACK IN SOUTH CAROLINA in October 1967, Sellers had his first encounter with historian Jack Bass, then the Columbia bureau chief for The Charlotte Observer and a stringer for The New York Times. Someone had suggested to Bass that he write a story about the civil rights organizer who was promoting black consciousness and advocating for black-studies programs. "You could tell he had been through a lot," recalled Bass.

In Orangeburg, Sellers continued his work with the Black Awareness Coordinating Committee at South Carolina State College. The NAACP had set up a student chapter there and was considered the primary civil rights group on campus. Sellers hoped to spark interest in black history and African history at the college, located just 30 miles northeast from his hometown. He was settling down and finding an audience. His mother was glad to have him nearby. South Carolina State had been established in 1896 as the state's only public college for blacks and as a land-grant institution providing agricultural and mechanical training. The state's all-white legislature provided financial support over the decades in an attempt to implement the "separate but equal" doctrine established by the U.S. Supreme Court in Plessy v. Ferguson. In the 1950s and 1960s, as blacks throughout the South began to demand their rights under the Constitution, the campus had been the scene of several student-led protests.

Sellers found a large group of students who welcomed him to campus. It was not unfamiliar territory for him. Many of the students knew about SNCC and many admired Sellers for his commitment to the movement, for his worldly outlook, for his big afro,

calm disposition and proud demeanor. They knew he had collab-
orated with Martin Luther King and Stokely Carmichael, that he
had organized voter registration drives in Mississippi, marched in
Alabama and debated Malcolm X. And some also knew that Sellers
had provided critical support for "The Cause," a student-led push
to remove the college's president, Benner C. Turner, earlier that
year and to pressure the school to hire more black contractors
and vendors. Sellers had helped student leaders set up the black
awareness coordinating commitee. Other students, though, were
reticent and kept their distance from this relatively famous agitator. For them, middle-class values and aspirations prompted the
expression of inherently moderate political views in order to rein-
force the social class to which educated African Americans (and
others) hoped to belong. Calls for radical change would upset the
social order and therefore potentially compromise the slow gains
made by some blacks.

But Sellers was not in Orangeburg to organize rebellions; he
wanted to raise consciousness, to convince students to demand
a systematic approach to black studies and to study a little himself. He discovered, however, that calling attention to academic
agendas that might advance the cause of the Black Power movement was a little like warning people busy with their umbrellas in
a rainstorm about the distant tsunami and its inexorable approach.
Many students still were preoccupied with the old agenda of fighting segregation in public establishments. They were focused on
the white-owned All Star Bowling Lanes on Russell Street that
remained segregated in 1968, nearly four years after the passage of
the Civil Rights Act. Sellers viewed the bowling alley as a problem
not worth confronting, not now, not when there were bigger fish
to fry, but the students around him were fixated on this rankling
offense and he was not going to stand in the way of legitimate protest, however ill-timed. "I don't try to keep anybody from using

any form of protest they want to use," he said. "If you want to demonstrate over the bowling alley, you have a right to do that. But I thought we were on the right track with identity and internationalism. That was kind of where I was, in terms of my thinking." Whites and middle-class blacks in the Orangeburg area were getting nervous about all the activity, and all this new talk about Black Power. The owner of the local bowling alley refused to admit blacks—despite the presence of two black colleges in town, despite the passage of the 1964 Civil Rights Act and despite public challenges and changes in public attitudes. The business had become the local symbol of segregation, and it prompted objections from students and civil rights activists.

IN EARLY 1968, the situation came to a head. For days, students demanded that the management lift its ban on blacks. The protest was part of a continuum of demonstrations by students from South Carolina State and from Claflin College, a historically black liberal arts college also located in downtown Orangeburg. Sellers was in Columbia on February 5, visiting Howard Levy, an Army captain and medical doctor, who was in the stockade at Fort Jackson for refusing to go to Vietnam. He also met with university students. "The University of South Carolina had a coffee house there and you would go there and meet these anti-war people," Sellers said. "I would go up there just to talk to that group." Arriving back in Orangeburg on February 6, he went straight to his home near campus. That evening, students who had been at All Star Bowling Lanes knocked on his door to inform him of the protests underway, asking that he go see for himself. "When I got there, there must have been 200 students down there," he said. "I went around to ask what people thought."

The situation had devolved from one of well-intended protest to something verging on a melee. John Stroman, a student leader at South Carolina State College receiving support from the local NAACP, spearheaded the protest, at one point entering the business with about 30 other students, as if this were a 1960 sit-in. In a moment of sympathy with the students, J.P. "Pete" Strom, chief of the State Law Enforcement Division (SLED), advised Stroman that if one or two of them could get arrested, it would be sufficient to trigger a court challenge to the bowling alley's segregation policy. The student leader encouraged most of his colleagues to return to campus; 15 submitted to arrest. Word soon reached other South Carolina State students watching a movie in the auditorium that there had been arrests at the bowling alley. Students streamed out and made a beeline for the protest site just a few blocks away. A cool-down might have been possible. The authorities were not yet overly confrontational, and the students were succeeding in making their point. But Orangeburg Police Chief Roger Poston called a fire truck to the scene, and that triggered memories of a 1960 sit-in during which fire hoses were turned on Claflin and South Carolina State students.

Now, the students began to jeer and taunt. "Hey man, where's the fire?" one shouted. Others ignited cigarette lighters. The authorities called for reinforcements, who arrived in riot gear. Stroman urged his fellow students to leave, but soon they were breaking windows and rocking police cars. One student sprayed liquefied tear gas into the eyes of a police officer. Police began beating the students with billy clubs. Protesters, many bloodied, quickly retreated to campus, throwing rocks through shop windows and damaging property at car dealerships along the way. Governor Robert McNair learned of the unrest and called for about 250 National Guardsmen to report to Orangeburg for standby duty. Strom, meanwhile, assigned

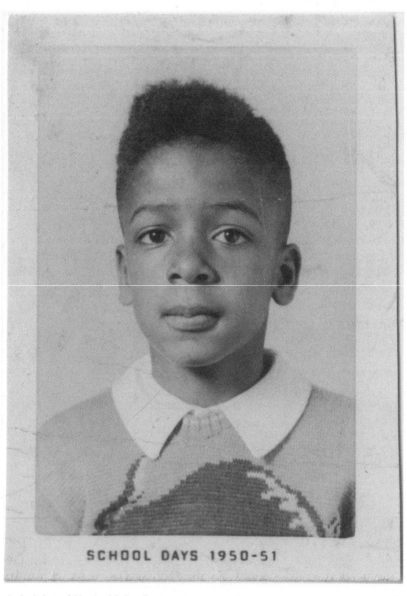

A school photo of Cleveland Sellers Jr. at age 6.

(Above) Sellers (center) at his sister's birthday party in Denmark, South Carolina, in 1951. (Below) Sellers with his beloved pony, riding through in Denmark in the late 1950s.

Sellers, at age 19, consults with white activists in the summer of 1964. SNCC and CORE had organized a massive voter registration drive in Mississippi dubbed "Freedom Summer," and Sellers was a SNCC Leader stationed in Holly Springs.

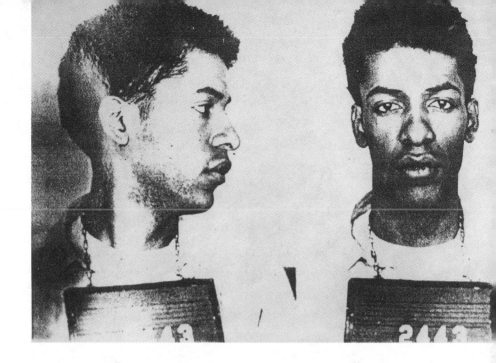

(Above) *A police mug shot of Cleveland Sellers after an early arrest. (Below) Sellers with Julian Bond, when both were members of the Student Nonviolent Coordinating Committee. Bond was communications director during his time with the organization.*

(Above) Sellers (left), King and Carmichael, with two others, during the Meredith March.
(Below) Sellers (background) with Martin Luther King Jr. and others at the state
capitol in Montgomery, Alabama, at the conclusion of the Meredith March in 1966.

Sellers with Martin Luther King Jr. and many others at the 1966 Meredith March for Freedom in Mississippi.

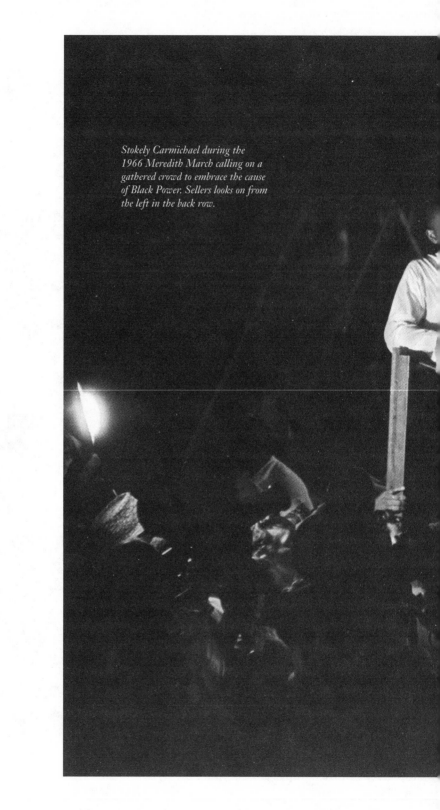

Stokely Carmichael during the 1966 Meredith March calling on a gathered crowd to embrace the cause of Black Power. Sellers looks on from the left in the back row.

Stokely Carmichael and Sellers shooting pool in Atlanta during a little down time in 1967.

Sellers on the night of February 8, 1968, leaving the Orangeburg County Courthouse following his arrest on riot charges after the campus shootings at South Carolina State College. At left is J.P. (Pete) Strom, chief of the South Carolina Law Enforcement Division. At right are Orangeburg County Chief Deputy B.N. Collins and Sheriff R.F. (Bob) Dukes. In the background are two unidentified SLED agents.

(Above) Sellers, in Atlanta with Stokely Carmichael, refuses induction in the U.S. military in 1967.

Sellers with fellow SNCC activist James Forman at a press conference in the second half of the 1960s.

(Left) Sellers with Charles Neblett, founder of the Freedom Singers, and Stokely Carmichael in Boston, in the mid-1960s.

Sellers (second from left) with Howard Fuller, at the 1969 grand opening of Malcolm X Liberation University in Durham, North Carolina. Malcolm's widow, Betty Shabazz, is seated at right.

Cast Your VOTE For
HOPE, TRUST and COMMITMENT

VOTE CLEVELAND SELLERS
District #1 City Council

PUNCH #27   **NOV. 8, 1983**

LET YOUR VOTE ADDRESS THESE CONCERNS:

OUR YOUTH- school dropouts, expulsion rate, youthful offenders, drug abuse, child abuse, hopelessness

OUR ELDERLY- decent housing, adequate protection, availability of city services, aggressive government representation

OUR COMMUNITY- adequate low-income housing, crime control, drug abuse, child care, voter registration, progressive representation, no hazardous landfills, unity

OUR FUTURE- community return to hope, commitment, involvement; availability of council person; organizing to defeat Senator Jesse Helms; increasing city support of black businesses; supporting goals and objectives of A&T, Bennett, and other black institutions; supporting each other

For Rides to the Polls, Call: 274-9667

(Left) Cleveland Sellers outside the prison where he served time in 1973. (Right) In 1983 Sellers ran for Greensboro City Council and lost to Earl Jones.

(Left) A 1969 article on the push for black studies on college campuses featured Sellers, who was lecturing at Cornell University at the time.

The New York Times Magazine APRIL 6, 1969

Battles ov classes an the Ithac partly ob may be th significan ment in A studies on in the cou left, Cleve Sellers, a SNCC org conducts in black l

Cornell's experience indicates why, all over the country, so much stress is being put on
The Black Studies Thing
By ERNEST DUNBAR

(Above) Sellers visiting the University of Virginia, with Martha Norman and Julian Bond, in 1994. (Below) SNCC veterans H. Rap Brown, Sellers, Judy Richardson and Courtland Cox, pictured at a Mississippi Freedom Summer reunion in Jackson, Mississippi, in 1984.

Sellers is now retired and living in Denmark, SC.

blame for the violence to Sellers, declaring, falsely, that the SNCC activist had stood on the hood of a car to address students and single-handedly directed the rebellion. "From then on it became a serious matter," Sellers said.

The next day, Wednesday, February 7, Sellers attended a campus grievance meeting at which incoming 35-year-old college President M. Maceo Nance, angered by the previous day's police actions, suggested a boycott of the city's commercial district, in part to keep students on campus. White business leaders and the mayor soon showed up, and the gathering degenerated into animosity when students thought they heard someone use the n-word. Though the city's white leadership said they would consider the students' grievances, tensions had not been defused. Sellers, leaning against the back wall, watched the proceedings with a sense of déjà vu, silently amused at the discomfort of the white officials and appalled by their tone-deafness. "They had no idea how to talk to people," he said, recalling the meeting. Sellers also was disappointed that the impassioned debate had to do with securing march permits (yet again) rather than advancing a Black Power agenda. Indeed, students produced a list of grievances for city hall that afternoon that, in addition to a call to shutter the bowling alley, expressed concerns about police brutality, health care discrimination, district gerrymandering and segregated drive-in theaters. In Orangeburg, at this late date, blacks were still fighting just to get in the door.

On Wednesday evening, with the city now on lockdown, a few Claflin students hopped a fence and cut through someone's back-yard near Russell Street to get to a sandwich shop. It was a route often taken, but this time the property owner, warned to be on the lookout for black mauraderes, fired his shotgun at the young people, striking some with birdshot. Police seemed to want to keep an eye on Sellers. Four patrol cars, with two policemen in each one, were parked in front of his house across College Avenue.

The proximity of the police intimidated Sellers, who stayed in a
dorm room on campus that night. Late the next morning, Sellers
noticed that the patrol cars had left, and he made his way back
home. When a TV news crew showed up at the house to interview
him, Sellers commented on the tense atmosphere. "Everybody is
looking for a scapegoat," he said on camera, adding that SNCC
was not directing student actions but that Stokely Carmichael
"probably will come to Orangeburg if they incarcerate me." It was
a veiled threat, an effort to convince the police to leave him alone.

Governor McNair, concerned about the potential for more
property damage and injury, and resentful of black militants,
feared an all-out urban riot, a mini-Detroit, and was determined to
pre-empt any such development. He activated 110 more National
Guardsmen. SLED Chief Strom oversaw squads of state troopers
gathered on the perimeter of campus. Agitated students, hyper-
aware of the militarized environment, felt stymied. As darkness fell
on Thursday, they decided to light a bonfire at the edge of campus.
To fuel the fire, they broke street signs, window shutters and pieces
of wood from a construction site and threw the material into the
blaze. It was a cold evening, with temperatures dipping below 30
degrees Fahrenheit. Then, in a classic case of escalating confrontation—where fear accumulates and no one in a position of authority
works to diffuse it and restore equilibrium—law enforcement officers gathered in greater numbers near the entrance to the campus
on orders to prevent marauding students from wreaking havoc in
the city; students, in turn, chastised their armed adversaries with
taunts and thrown objects. Just after 9 p.m., someone fired a .22
caliber gun from the nearby Claflin campus, aiming over the heads
of patrolmen positioned on College Avenue. Soon after, a patrolman fired a riot gun into the air as a warning. Students noticed a
prison transport van from the Department of Corrections parked
nearby, ready in case of mass arrests. Sellers, concerned for his

own safety, remained in the dormitory. Students—about 200 this time—rekindled the bonfire in an act of defiance, singing civil rights songs and jeering at police. By then, the bowling alley had closed, the campus was under lockdown and police had stopped traffic into downtown Orangeburg. Military vehicles were stationed at strategic intersections near campus. The situation was ominous.

JUST BEFORE 10:30 P.M., Strom and other officers stationed at the corner of College Avenue and Russell Street decided to call for a fire truck to douse the bonfire and prevent students from throwing objects set aflame in the direction of troopers or vulnerable property. As the siren wailed, the fire truck drove slowly toward the bonfire and a group of patrolmen moved with it to offer protection. Sellers heard the siren and left the dormitory to see what was happening. Some students were in retreat; others were cursing the patrolmen. Someone hurled two banisters toward the officers, and one struck Patrolman David Shealy in the face. "Shealy's been shot!" a patrolman yelled, observing his colleague's bloodied face. The situation was now a recipe for disaster. There was no clear command structure. The bonfire had been doused, but that did little to temper the agitation among jittery law enforcement officials. Confrontational students resorted to nasty epithets.

Sellers decided to approach a group of students to warn them of the danger they faced and to encourage them to clear the area. State troopers were positioned at the edge of campus by College Avenue, close to the bonfire. They were armed with buckshot rather than less-lethal birdshot. The atmosphere was thick with fear and anger as students clustered nearby along Watson Street, the small road between College Avenue and campus. After issuing his initial warning, Sellers noticed that the bonfire was out and that a security officer was positioned on a nearby corner. He figured things had calmed down, he said. "I crossed the street toward the gathering. I noticed [the troopers] had their guns drawn." Recognizing student Henry Smith, he thought, "I have to get these people out of here." He started to make his way toward Smith. "And that's when the guns went off."

At about 10:30 p.m., one of the 66 patrolmen assigned to the scene fired warning shots into the air, triggering panic and prompting nine close-by officers ill-trained in crowd-control techniques who, now pointing their shotguns at the mass of vulnerable bodies just up the bluff, fired their weapons. Students fell all around him, Sellers recalled. He heard people shout, "I'm shot! I'm hurt! Somebody help me!" So he raced to the embankment where injured students writhed in pain and fear. He tried to help one, and then another who seemed worse off, hoping to carry him to the infirmary. Then Sellers was hit. "I felt a hot burning sensation and it turned my body," he recalled. Buckshot had struck him near the armpit. "I was doing one of those belly flops. Besides the burning, I still had the ability to move, and even move that arm. So I knew the first thing to do was get out of there. They might come up with flashlights looking for someone who looked like me, so I couldn't jump up and run." He shuffled back across State Street and hid behind a tree, then a garbage can. Other young men scrambled desperately to escape the bombardment, clawing their way up the embankment further into the campus. Many were shot in the back, side or feet as they turned to flee or fell to the ground. Several were hit multiple times by the large pellets that tore easily through their flesh.

It all happened so quickly. The shooting lasted only about ten seconds. One student recalled seeing the flashes emanating from the ends of the patrolmen's shotguns. Another assumed the gunfire was directed over the heads of the students as a fear tactic until he noticed his friends dropping injured to the ground. One young man was struck in the face, the pellet knocking out 16 teeth and slicing his tongue in two. In the end, two South Carolina State students—Henry Smith and Samuel Hammond—and one Wilkinson High School student, Delano Middleton, were killed; at least 28 others were injured. Hammond was shot in the back. Middleton was shot seven times, one pellet piercing his heart. Smith, who was positioned close to the firing squad, was struck five times, including once behind the right shoulder, the slug exiting his body through the left side of his neck. Sellers thought the patrolmen would advance up the hill and further into the campus. He thought maybe they were coming for him. The troopers shooting into the crowd had not heard an order to fire; others soon shouted commands to stop. But it wasn't until Patrolman James R. Powers blew his whistle that the shooting began to slow, then cease. Sellers quickly returned to the bloody side of the street to help move injured students to the infirmary. Some found their own way there; others had to be carried. A single nurse, Bernice Daniels, was quickly overwhelmed. Faculty members and other students rushed to help and, because no ambulances were immediately present, to drive the wounded to the still segregated Orangeburg Hospital.

Sellers went to the hospital to seek treatment and was sitting in the "colored waiting room" with other victims when a black deputy pointed him out to Orangeburg County Sheriff Robert Dukes, who took the SNCC activist into custody. Worried about what the authorities might do to him, Sellers announced loudly to everyone he passed on his way out, "Y'all see I'm going with the sheriff, the sheriff's got me."

The state brought riot-related charges against him, bond was set at $50,000, and Sellers was taken to the state penitentiary near Columbia. He had come home to South Carolina partly to get away from the intensifying pressures of SNCC's civil rights work—to get out of the line of fire—and now he was in jail again. He knew he had been only superficially involved in the student protests, that he was mostly an observer of a gathering storm who, despite his efforts to maintain focus on Black Power issues and act as a mentor to S.C. State and Claflin students, nevertheless found himself caught up in a tornado of terrible violence. And he was the one blamed for it. Cleveland Sellers Jr., 23, would pay a steep price and carry the burden of the Orangeburg Massacre with him for the rest of his life.

12 LEGAL WRANGLING, SNCC CHAOS

AFTER THE HORRORS of Orangeburg, authorities began building their case against Sellers, claiming he was the instigator. A grand jury quickly indicted him on charges of participating in a riot, incitement to riot and conspiracy to incite others to riot. Other charges—arson, housebreaking and grand larceny, assault and battery with intent to kill, destruction of personal property and damaging real property—failed to stick. While he awaited his criminal trial, Sellers was released from jail March 1, 1968, on a reduced bond of $20,000, and a promise not to come within five miles of Orangeburg.

Sellers quietly returned to Atlanta. He didn't feel safe in South Carolina. The press had vilified him as the outside agitator. The

FBI had colluded with other law enforcement agencies to sully his name. He and others were haunted by the thought that perhaps he had been the intended target of an assassination plot in Orangeburg, one that allegedly went awry when police mistook Henry Smith for Sellers. His mother, Pauline, worried that the bull's-eye he now wore on his back would make him the next martyr of the civil rights movement. He had gambled and lost. The campus atmosphere in which he had found himself was abuzz with pent-up anger and resentment, not the sort of determination that could drive the movement in South Carolina from its heroic phase of nonviolent resistance to a new phase of power sharing and self-sufficiency.

The movement, meanwhile, appeared to be tearing apart at the seams, adding strain to veterans already exhausted by circumstances. Sellers spent much of the spring and summer sharing a small Atlanta apartment with 25-year-old Willie Ricks, scrounging for food and rent money, and talking with students about black nationalism and other issues. It was an anxiety-ridden period. Left and right, Sellers' colleagues in the movement were coping with aggressive legal actions against them. Many were sent to prison, sometimes for minor offenses. Prison terms ranged from a couple of years to decades. Rap Brown was in the biggest trouble, along with the Panthers' Bobby Seale and Huey Newton. Brown had been charged in mid-1967 with inciting arson and riot in Cambridge, Maryland, followed up by firearms charges, bond violations and threatening FBI officers. Several others saddled with criminal charges were being hunted by law enforcement: Carmichael, Ricks, SNCC's new chairman Phil Hutchings, former SNCC operatives Lee Otis Johnson and Fred Brooks, among them. It was difficult to avoid concluding that the government had launched a deliberative campaign to eliminate or disable proponents of Black Power. Sellers felt as though he was on the run and eventually would end up in prison or dead.

Certainly law enforcement had reason to fear black radicals openly calling for rebellion. Most Americans, white and black, were no big fans of Black Power, and they were unable to differentiate between the new movement's two strains, one calling for a soft cultural revolution, the other calling for a militant political revolution. All they heard was the aggressive rhetoric, and that was enough for them to offer tacit support for—or at least tolerance of—increasingly harsh police tactics. The national backlash against the legal and cultural gains extracted by the civil rights movement of the 1950s and 1960s and the reactionary pushback from the country's establishment had begun in earnest. This initial roundup of militants was Phase One. The government had decided enough was enough.

A Department of Defense counter-intelligence report from 1967 reveals the concerns (and blind spots) of government observers:

> The growing popularity of H. Rap Brown, Stokely Carmichael, and SNCC indicates a changing temper in Negro racist agitation. More and more Negroes are accepting the SNCC policy of violence and destruction of established social order in the U.S. Recent utterances of SNCC leaders call for Negroes to arm themselves in preparation for guerrilla warfare to overthrow the "imperialist" government of the United States. They seek to destroy the present American economic, political, and social systems in a SNCC-defined attempt to gain "freedom" for the Negro.
>
> The growing discontent of Negroes in the United States creates an ideal situation for the propaganda of the hate-mongers of SNCC. The leaders are actively touring the country to preach their sermons of violence in Negro ghettos, where they constantly stress their concept of "Black Power."

SNCC, the report asserted, no longer could be classified as a civil rights group; it had become a racist organization whose members advocated black supremacy and expressed hatred for whites. In fact, SNCC was not pushing a supremacist agenda but, rather, one that expressed sympathies with other nationalistic movements around the globe that purportedly fought against *white* supremacy and Western imperialism. The new internationalist approach soon resulted in published SNCC statements on a variety of topics, including a strongly worded critique of Zionism and its impact on the Palestinians. This missive, perhaps more than any other, prompted and accelerated the withdrawal of financial support from SNCC—once-sympathetic American Jews and other liberals stopped sending in their checks. SNCC, now led by the more radical Rap Brown and renamed the Student National Coordinating Committee, teetered on bankruptcy. This was only the latest example of SNCC's primary dilemma playing itself out: Should the organization forego support from white allies in the interest of black self-determination, thereby putting its very survival at risk? On the other hand, perhaps the time for revolution was indeed at hand.

After the Orangeburg shootings, SNCC was too preoccupied with Rap Brown's legal troubles to pay Sellers much attention. The organization published a two-page statement about Orangeburg in an effort to set the record straight, but the often contradictory explanations offered by South Carolina officials and the press, especially in the immediate aftermath of the shootings, helped to ensure that those who were following the story couldn't quite discern the truth. Though Sellers had not encouraged the bowling alley protestors nor played an active role, he was nevertheless singled out as the culprit. "He's the main man," SLED spokesman Henry Lake said, accusing Sellers of throwing the banister that struck the trooper. "He's the biggest nigger in the crowd." It was only the latest repetition of falsehoods regarding Sellers' role: he did not throw the banister, he did not stand atop a police car and direct protestors, he did not lead the rebellion against the bowling alley and he did not encourage violence. Martin Luther King Jr. sent a formal written appeal to U.S. Attorney General Ramsey Clark: "We demand that you act now to bring to justice the perpetrators of the largest armed assault undertaken under color of law in recent Southern history." It did not help. Meanwhile, legal appeals in Sellers' case—and in related ones—pushed off his day of reckoning in the Orangeburg incident for two more years.

SELLERS' DRAFT-EVASION TRIAL started on March 29, 1968. He appeared in the courtroom of 56-year-old U.S. District Judge Newell Edenfield and before a jury of nine whites and three blacks. Julian Bond and John Lewis testified on Sellers' behalf, but to no avail. The jury found Sellers guilty, and Edenfield ordered the defendant to return in a month for sentencing. The following week, Sellers went to New York City to confront SNCC leader James Forman about the lack of support for his Orangeburg predicament and to raise awareness of the shooting. Then he headed to Washington, D.C., to join Carmichael, who was scheduled to give a speech on April 5 about the government's persecution of Rap Brown. When Sellers arrived at the airport on April 4, Carmichael, Bob Brown and Bill Hall were there waiting for him, strangely silent. A few SCLC people rushed past them, mumbling something about catching a flight to Memphis.

"We've got to go back downtown," to the SNCC office, Carmichael said to him.

Sellers was confused. "Will somebody tell me what's going on?" he demanded. King had been killed in Memphis, Tennessee. Sellers crumpled at the news.

"Dr. King had been [Sellers'] spiritual adviser on the conscientious objection hassle with the draft," Carmichael noted in his memoir. "He'd grown to even love Dr. King from the Meredith

March. I couldn't even look at Cleve, the brother was in such pain." That evening, Carmichael, Sellers, Ricks, Hall and Brown took to the streets to encourage business owners "to close as a sign of mourning and respect." By 11 p.m., tensions in the District gave way to a full-throated street rebellion. The next day, Carmichael addressed first the press, then a gathering of students at Howard University, warning them to "stay off the streets if you don't have a gun." Carmichael wanted to return to his apartment, to remain in the community during this troubled and terrifying moment. His new wife, South African singer Miriam Makeba, was there, having flown to D.C. from Los Angeles, too distraught by the assassination to perform at the Coconut Grove in Hollywood and worried sick about her husband. Sellers, ever the pragmatic revolutionary, argued that his friend's high profile and recent history of incendiary rhetoric made him a person of extreme interest to the FBI and local police, who would know where to find him and likely would go to some lengths to find an excuse to accuse the Black Power spokesman of contributing to the rioting. Or maybe something worse would happen. Maybe Carmichael would become the next target of assassination. Better, Sellers argued, to find a safe haven and friendly witnesses, to have an alibi. So Sellers, Carmichael, Hall and Mickey McGuire laid low. They spent a night in a suburban house owned by the Tanzanian government. Meanwhile looting and burning continued in the city, and the White House dispatched 15,000 federal troops to the streets.

After a few days, they drove to Atlanta to attend King's funeral, struggling to gain access to the sanctuary of Ebenezer Baptist Church, into which about 1,300 people, including a number of dignitaries and celebrities, squeezed. They positioned themselves by the entrance, then pushed in behind members of the King family, surprising the guards.

* ❋ *

KING'S DEATH CAME less than three months after the civil rights icon had performed the marriage rites for Sellers and Sandy Duncan. Sandy had come with Sellers to Orangeburg, had started singing with a local band and had wanted to help with the civil rights work. But she was not content, Sellers said. "She was a person who was sad a lot. I didn't figure it out until it was [too] late." At a New Year's party, during a trip to New York City, Sellers had become physically violent with her when he saw her talking with Rap Brown again. Maybe Sandy was right, maybe a wedding would help the relationship, he thought. Sellers had introduced Sandy to Dr. King at the Meredith March, and with Sandy pressuring him about marriage, Sellers cashed in a chip. "I called Dr. King and said, 'Sandy and I are going to get married, and you had already told me that I needed to do the right thing, so I want to know when I can come over to Atlanta.' I sent Stokely or Willie Ricks to the courthouse to get a license. So we went over to Atlanta, and Stokely was the best man." On January 24, in the basement of Ebenezer Baptist Church, King performed the marriage rites.

Two weeks later, there was pandemonium in Orangeburg, followed by legal maneuvering, fundraising and jail time. Sandy wasn't there for the state trooper shootings on the campus of South Carolina State College, but she came soon after to move their belongings out of the house they had rented adjacent to the campus. "By this time she is pretty much scared to death," Sellers said. Then King was assassinated. "And so I go down to Dr. King's funeral, and shortly after that, the federal judge called me back to court for sentencing, and they sentence me to five years, and at the same time use information from Orangeburg to deny me bond."

At his sentencing in late April, Sellers was defiant, still burning with anger and sorrow three weeks after the assassination. He knew what was at stake, he understood well the risks associated with his principled stance on the war and he had conditioned himself emotionally to absorb whatever blows he might receive in the courtroom. He thought of himself as a black militant, a victim of a system set against him and against the ideals of black empowerment. He had witnessed violent assaults against aggrieved black people committed in the interest of maintaining law and order. His courtroom rhetoric was no exaggeration. It was heartfelt. "This court can't sentence me," he declared. "I am a black man and this court is racist. The only people who can sentence me are black people, and I don't see any here. I will fight, as my black brothers have fought, for the liberation of black people, and I will fight to the death." Howard Moore tried to contextualize his client's heated comments, but a visibly enraged Edenfield would have none of it and doomed Sellers to five years in prison, the maximum sentence allowed.

Sellers was held briefly in the Fulton County Jail without bail because the court considered him a militant. Two days later he was moved to a jail in Newnan, Georgia; two days after that he was locked in a cell in Rome, Georgia, where he spent two and half weeks before being relocated to a federal prison in Tallahassee, Florida. Racial tensions ran high there. Though he resisted, prison officials shaved off Sellers' afro, which demoralized him. Blacks and whites brawled in the prison yard as Sellers watched from the small window of his cell. Administrators moved black and white prisoners into separate barracks and staggered mealtimes to minimize interaction. Then Sellers was shipped out to the federal penitentiary in Terre Haute, Indiana, where he spent about three months. He was scared. Received as a black agitator who had reportedly instigated the Tallahassee brawl and the Orangeburg Massacre, Sellers was warned by the warden and guards to stay in line.

In late August, he was sent back to Atlanta, and Moore petitioned U.S. Supreme Court Justice Hugo Black for his release, pointing out that Sellers always showed up in court, and that even in the Orangeburg case, the judge thought it proper to release him on bail. Rejecting the lower court's reasoning for refusing to issue a bond, Black ordered that a bond not in excess of $5,000 be made available. Black felt Sellers' refusal to renounce violence as a means of self-defense was a First Amendment matter of free speech, and his incarceration without bail was unfair, Moore later said. On August 22, the Atlanta Superior Court judge then set bail at $2,500 and, after four months behind bars, Sellers walked free. He and his attorneys, along with the American Civil Liberties Union, would continue to appeal the decision and the case would drag on for three years until charges ultimately were dismissed on June 22, 1971. His marriage, however, did not survive the stint in prison. He had asked a friend in New York City to look after Sandy while he sat in jail. She moved around a lot and soon became romantically entangled with activist George Ware. Sellers learned of the affair after he was released, but by then he was not willing to fight for her. "I didn't get a divorce. I just said I had to move on."

IN THE WAKE OF KING'S MURDER, black activists were in the throes of significant introspection and realignment. SNCC's internationalism and the Black Panthers' militant domestic agenda often were difficult to reconcile. The Panthers had sprung like Eve from the rib of SNCC, and Carmichael, Forman and Rap Brown had been made honorary Panther members that February. But internal conflict came to a head at a July 1968 meeting in New York City to organize a rally at the United Nations. While Sellers was in prison, they planned to call a U.N. plebiscite in support of the black struggle and to draw attention to the legal troubles of Rap Brown and Panther leader Huey Newton. But the real subject of the meeting was the tenuous and unofficial alliance between the two organizations. SNCC leaders objected to the idea of a merger, insisting that their colleagues renounce any affiliation with the Panthers. Forman and Brown complied with the demand, but not Carmichael. And when controversy erupted over leadership and management, the Panthers threatened Forman with violence.

In September, Carmichael was unceremoniously kicked out of SNCC when he refused to resign from his honorary position with the Black Panthers. That December, at a meeting in Atlanta over which Forman presided, Sellers and Ricks—both closely associated with the Black Power firebrand—were dismissed after refusing to help with another merger scheme, this time between SNCC and the small, militant St. Louis-based group called The Liberators. Ricks and Sellers considered the openly revolutionary stance of the group self-defeating. The Atlanta gathering degenerated into threats and menace. The two men argued that they still were interested in building community and working with organizations dedicated to political and economic empowerment, but they were strongly opposed to mergers of convenience with paramilitary groups. "We didn't think that was the most prudent and positive thing we could do," Sellers reflected. "We saw what was happening with the Black Panther Party....When you say you have a gun, you actually create more tension, and give police an excuse [to exercise their power]."

The next afternoon, Sellers was in the waiting area of his attorney Howard Moore's office when four men arrived, demanded to know why he was trying to destroy SNCC, then began to beat him. Sellers was not trying to destroy SNCC; in his view, the organization already had been destroyed. The moment was fraught with peril. Sellers wondered if the men were associated in some way, directly or indirectly, with the FBI. After all, government agents had succeeded by 1968 in worming their way into several civil rights and leftist groups, and they had identified individuals who seemed to embrace revolutionary militancy as well as others, like Sellers, who resisted overtly calling for violence. For agents seeking to destroy the Black Power movement, it was easier to justify going after armed rebels, Sellers noted. Those who were less radical—like him—were inconvenient obstacles.

"I was certain there were FBI agents infiltrating around the perimeter of SNCC," Sellers said. "I didn't know whether [my assailants] were agents. I was trying to figure out real quick whether they were coming to beat me up and send a message to people who resist." As blows rained down upon him, Sellers gathered his strength and pushed the four men away, noticing a big gun fall from one of their pockets to the floor. He pulled out his own .38 caliber pistol and was preparing to fire when Moore entered the room and talked him down. The men fled.

It was all so anticlimactic, so disappointing. All those years of hard work, all that sacrifice so that SNCC might continue to be a force for social change. But the tide had turned. To be fired from SNCC because of petty infighting was for Sellers a pathetic, almost comical, end to his long association with the once-noble organization.

13 ## THE TRIALS

THE SOUTH CAROLINA State College shootings had infuriated black activists, who mostly learned of the disastrous confrontation through the grapevine, black media and academic channels. Mainstream media largely downplayed or ignored the shootings. The Associated Press initially mischaracterized the violence, claiming there was "a heavy exchange of gunfire" between troopers and students, then never properly corrected the mistake. SNCC and other civil rights organizations quickly published condemnations. The debacle, which soon came to be known as the Orangeburg Massacre—a reference to the 1960 Sharpeville Massacre of South Africa which killed 69 and wounded 180—was the first deadly campus shooting involving law enforcement in the United States.

A nervous Sellers suspected that he had been the real target in Orangeburg, that troopers were firing into the crowd of students partly because they had been implicitly encouraged to shoot him. There was no evidence for this theory, but that did nothing to assuage Sellers' concerns, expressed forcefully in a short interview published in Columbia's The State newspaper upon his release from jail. "I'll have to talk with my people in this state," Sellers told reporter Sam McCuen. "I don't plan to be scared out of South Carolina. This is my home. They tried to murder me at Orangeburg and scare me out. It was a disservice for the governor to send his Klansmen in disguise to do the killing on order. I'd call that trying to scare me out of the state. They were shooting at me. I still can't go back to Orangeburg. But I have a home there. They can't keep me from wanting to go back, though. It's not over down there yet."

AT THE TIME of the Orangeburg Massacre, the late Matthew J. Perry Jr., senior U.S. District Judge in Columbia with a courthouse now named for him, was an attorney serving on the national board of the NAACP. He also was chairman of the state legal committee of the South Carolina NAACP branch and had represented more than 6,000 defendants. He had met Sellers' aunt in Spartanburg, where he was starting his law practice as a young man. "I came to know the family and, through her, the family's involvement in community affairs," Perry recalled. Perry and the NAACP leadership had been aware of the ban on blacks at the All Star Bowling Lanes. In fact, he had gone to Orangeburg before the shootings to confer with residents about taking legal action. "I indicated a willingness to be of assistance if there were people willing to challenge the bowling alley," he said. "Technically, we had to be invited in." On the night of the shootings Perry had received a phone call in the middle of the night: "Did you know police are killing students down there in Orangeburg?" the voice said. "I was devastated, I was shocked," Perry said. Immediately, he began to consult over the phone with colleagues. "All of us became, let's say, animated."

Howard Moore, the Atlanta-based attorney preferred by SNCC, called Perry to ask if he would oversee the investigation and arrange to free Sellers on bail. "Almost immediately, I went over to the state penitentiary to see him. He was glad to see me.... I was convinced he had done no wrong," Perry remembered. But the internal politics of the civil rights movement pervaded even Sellers' jail cell. "My folks don't like you," Sellers told Perry during that first visit, referring to SNCC. The young militants preaching Black Power and advocating direct action considered Perry an insider, part of the establishment, and associated with an organization often disparaged for its moderation. So Perry ultimately stayed out of the way of the defense team, led by Moore, providing only unofficial assistance, he said.

DURING THE SPRING of 1969, nine South Carolina state patrolmen went to trial in the Orangeburg Massacre case. The jury included 10 whites and two blacks. "[The defense's] strategy was to try to make sure any black juror selected had little education, came from a rural area, and belonged to no civil rights organizations," wrote Jack Bass and Jack Nelson in *The Orangeburg Massacre*. Sellers had not been subpoenaed to testify, neither by the prosecution nor by the defense. Government prosecutors assumed Sellers' lawyer would recommend that he invoke the Fifth Amendment, or that he would exaggerate the facts in a show of Black Power; defense attorneys, who had had no contact with Sellers, feared he would contradict testimony that supported the patrolmen.

The trial revealed many important facts and nuances about the campus shooting, from the number of law enforcement officials in Orangeburg on that day (127 patrolmen and 450 National Guardsmen, 66 of the former and 45 of the latter at the campus) to the verbal exchanges between belligerent students and troopers. Details about the confrontation at the bowling alley on February 6 also were described, including the concerns of J.P. "Pete" Strom, chief of the State Law Enforcement Division. Strom testified that the situation at the bowling alley deteriorated once Sellers appeared on the scene.

"Did you know him before then, Chief?" asked Frank Taylor, the defense attorney.

"I knew who he was," Strom replied. "I knew that he was representing the Atlanta Division of the Student Nonviolent Coordinating Committee hooked up with Rap Brown, Stokely Carmichael, and that crowd. I knew that much about him and we had been keeping up with that group." Lawyers for the defense asked student witnesses about Sellers, clearly hoping the testimony would reveal that the civil rights activist had orchestrated the student rebellion, at least in part, but no evidence was presented proving, or even suggesting, that Sellers had played an active role.

FBI agents testified that they believed shots had been fired from the campus somewhere and that the shotgun blasts from troopers had come in response. Taylor called for a not-guilty verdict, arguing that "militants coming into South Carolina and inciting students" was the true cause of the tragic unrest. Students, he said, must respect law and order. "If you convict anybody in this case, how would you ever get a highway patrolman, deputy sheriff, city policeman, or anybody to serve if the state didn't back them up? It's your duty to back up these men," he told the jury. And that's exactly what the jury did. The basic legal question was whether the shootings constituted self-defense: Did the nine defendants believe they were in imminent danger when they decided to fire their weapons, and would an ordinary person have felt endangered in similar circumstances? The jurors took one hour and 42 minutes to decide a verdict of not guilty. For Sellers, it was a demoralizing blow.

As the trial was underway, Sellers was starting what would eventually become a full-fledged academic career. That spring, he was invited to spend a semester as a visiting lecturer at Cornell University, an early adopter of a distinct black studies program (the first was San Francisco State University). It was a good opportunity to get away from the South, to do something new. Little did Sellers know that Cornell was itself a hotbed of racial unrest and that he would end up offering advice to protesting students who wanted the school to hire more African Americans (and pay them better) and to improve the black studies program. He lectured on black ideologies during the spring semester, all the while paying occasional visits to North Carolina to help Howard Fuller, an educator from Milwaukee, Wisconsin, start up a new school, Malcolm X Liberation University. Sometimes he brought his Cornell students with him, encouraging them to embrace a pan-African outlook and hoping they might be inspired to teach at the fledgling school once they earned their degrees from Cornell.

FINALLY, ON SEPTEMBER 24, 1970, it came time for Sellers' criminal trial. An Orangeburg County courtroom filled with highway patrolmen, black students and other onlookers as Circuit Court Judge John Grimball of Charleston and a jury of nine whites and three blacks heard the case against the 25-year-old man accused of provoking a riot and of playing a leading role in the mayhem. "Sellers arrived in the court room at 9:45 a.m., 15 minutes after court was scheduled to open," wrote Frank K. Myers in the The Times & Democrat of Orangeburg. "He wore an Afro-style haircut, brown bell-bottom trousers and a figured dashiki."

In the indictment, Sellers had been charged with riot only for the night of February 8, the night of the killings. On the witness stand, 10 law enforcement officers interrogated by the prosecution could not link Sellers to the February 8 campus confrontation, except to affirm that he was among those wounded by buckshot. The judge set aside the charge of inciting a riot and conspiracy to incite a riot. But relying on a bit of tortured legal logic, he directed the jury to consider for the riot charge only the events of February 6, the day of the bowling alley protest, during which students damaged shops and cars. The defense moved for an acquittal, citing the irregularity, but the judge ruled an imprecise indictment was permissible, though no hard evidence had been presented demonstrating Sellers' involvement in the confrontations of February 6. Orangeburg Police Chief Roger Poston testified that he had seen him "move from group to group" outside the bowling alley, but noticed no illegal behavior, according to an account in New South magazine. After two hours of deliberation, the jury returned a guilty verdict on the riot charge. Grimball gave Sellers the maximum sentence of one year in jail and fined him $250. An appeals bond of $5,000 was set and immediately paid. Sellers was free to go.

Moore, a mild-mannered if thorough and dogged civil rights attorney, was furious that the judge had not set aside the riot change and directed an acquittal. There simply was no evidence. "I'm not surprised in the least bit," he declared outside the courtroom. "Black people believe they can't get a fair trial in racist America and this was proven today in Orangeburg." He scoffed at the prosecution's stubborn assertion that his client had participated in the Orangeburg violence, an allegation maintained despite the lack of evidence. "[This was] the first one-man riot in history," Moore said.

Sellers and his parents were more sanguine, showing little emotion. "I've seen it happen too many times before," Pauline Sellers said with a sigh as she left the Orangeburg courthouse. Cleveland

Sellers was even more resigned. "The veterans of the Civil Rights Movement kind of knew from Mississippi and Alabama that we weren't going to be able to win a case in state court," he said. He recalled how some judges hardly paid attention to attorneys presenting evidence or making their arguments. It seemed they had already decided to convict the black defendants. "I knew there was little or no chance that we were going to get out of there as innocent," Sellers said. "If they were going to allow that to happen, they would have let the case ride out [or] not prosecute." It was Governor McNair who insisted on prosecuting Sellers, and that sent a clear signal to both sides, Sellers said. When reporters approached him afterwards, he was blunt. He called it a kangaroo court.

Appeals went on for more than two years, finally reaching the U.S. Supreme Court, which announced in a precedent-setting decision, that an indictment's reference to the timing of an alleged crime could be imprecise. Sellers would have to go to jail.

THOUGH LAW ENFORCEMENT officials and federal agencies have scrutinized the events of the Orangeburg shootings, no formal state investigation has ever been conducted. Historian Jack Bass, Sellers and many others have long called for such an investigation. "Is there anyone in South Carolina who believes that if three students were killed and 28 had been wounded in 1968 by police gunfire on the campus of the University of South Carolina or Clemson, that the state wouldn't have had a full investigation and report to the people of South Carolina?" Bass asked.

Governor McNair, who died in 2007, remained unconvinced by Sellers' arguments for the rest of his life. He never abandoned the idea that Sellers' meddling had caused the violence, though he called the confrontation "a scar on our state's conscience." He also felt that it had sullied his political legacy and derailed his career because it undermined his contention that South Carolina was a moderate state when it came to race relations. In the summer of 1968, he had been one of four people Democratic presidential candidate Hubert Humphrey was considering for vice president. He was chairman of both the Southern Governors Conference and the National Democratic Governors Conference. McNair was well connected, influential and, like Humphrey, had a reputation for pragmatism, and he was proud of South Carolina's improved political and economic standings. In the spring of 1967 he had successfully intervened in an earlier, potentially combustible episode of social unrest on the campus of South Carolina State College. But at the Democratic convention that August, the subject of the Orangeburg Massacre came up. Alonzo W. Holman, president of the South Carolina State NAACP and a delegate to the convention, told an aid to Humphrey that he no longer could support McNair. In the end, Edmund S. Muskie of Maine was named the vice presidential nominee.

FORTY-SIX YEARS AFTER the campus shootings at South Carolina State, Sellers' youngest child, Bakari Sellers, was asked by Julian Bond about the episode and how it affected his father. The younger Sellers, then a 30-year-old politician relinquishing his seat in the South Carolina House of Representatives to run for lieutenant governor, was a rising star in the Democratic Party who provided intelligent insights into race relations. He would lose his bid for lieutenant governor but soon become a paid CNN analyst, which gave him a national profile and helped set the stage for future public service. "I think that I'm angrier about February 8 than he is," Bakari Sellers told Bond. "I think he's come to some reconciliation within his own heart about that day. But it was a day that will forever stain the history of our great state....And there remain a lot of unanswered questions about what actually happened that day."

The younger Sellers praised the students at South Carolina State who confronted the intransigent owner of the bowling alley. "That gumption, that courage, that audacity for them to believe that they could break down that last barrier of segregation in South Carolina just showed the strength of that young generation," he said. But their courage was met with fire power, and this disrupted a narrative popular among white politicians and civic leaders at the time. Governor McNair portrayed the state as a exception in the Deep South, a place that, unlike Mississippi or Louisiana, could boast of a lack of racial violence and confrontation. "February 8 blew that up, and I think, as well, blew up his chances to be vice president of the United States," Sellers said.

The shootings, though a watershed moment for South Carolina, are little known and poorly understood, Bakari Sellers pointed out. "You don't hear about South Carolina State, but two years later everyone knows about Kent State," he said. "And I truly believe that if the lessons were learned from Orangeburg that we could have saved a number of lives." The injustices of Orangeburg, especially the way they impacted his father, motivated the young Sellers to pursue a career in law, he told Bond. "That egged me on in my legal career, because I kind of understood how the judiciary system kind of yanked him around, and the criminal justice system didn't quite do justice until 25 years later."

14 ENTERING A NEW LIFE

BY THE TIME Sellers was ejected from SNCC, he harbored few illusions about the status and potential of the organization. Its personnel had changed; its mission had lost its insight and focus; its finances were in shambles; its allies had disappeared and; worst of all, it no longer could tap into a dominant strain of national discontent. Cast to the sidelines of the global freedom struggle, SNCC had become what any social justice organizer most fears: ineffective.

Sellers was not among those who endorsed the violent overthrow of the status quo; he was a cultural revolutionary. He wanted to celebrate African heritage. He wanted African Americans to become enlightened students of history who could simultaneously exude cultural pride and participate in the full promise of American citizenship, to see themselves as sufficient, whole. He also wanted to keep learning and to keep teaching, this time in a formal university setting, but that would not be possible in South Carolina. He had been warned not to return.

In the fall of 1969 he enrolled at Harvard (despite lacking an undergraduate degree, for he had abandoned Howard University for the life of an activist before securing one) where he earned a master's degree in education. There, too, black students were rebelling, and there, too, Sellers assumed his activist-advisor role, even taking a place at the negotiating table across from Archibald Cox, who represented Harvard's interests. Like students elsewhere, Harvard's protestors wanted more black faculty, students and workers on campus and a stronger black studies program. After about 10 days of on-and-off negotiations, a compromise was achieved: the school agreed to develop and execute a new recruitment plan. Though he applied himself to his studies, worked hard and communicated regularly with his professors, Sellers could not keep away from the racial issues on campus. "There's something in your bones when you see young people trying to engage in social activism that pulls you in that direction," he said.

It was a relief to be away from SNCC and the Southern civil rights movement. "It gave me a chance to slow down and do stuff I wanted to do," he said. "I liked my time in that education environment. It was one of the most unique I've experienced." He was intellectually engaged. He enjoyed using the well-equipped and well-appointed libraries. He respected his professors, especially since many of them had public policy experience. "SNCC had trained me how to ask the questions that you wanted answered. It was an awesome experience that got me sharp again in terms of concepts and ideas and the importance of books and reading and writing. It really made me curious, even more so."

But all along, Seller knew he wanted to live and work in the South. Greensboro, North Carolina, was the place that appealed to him. Sellers was intrigued by the city's sense of itself, and by the prominent and dynamic black community. He knew of its activism; appreciated the historically black North Carolina A&T State University; remembered well the Woolworth lunch counter sit-ins which, in 1960, had prompted thousands of students, including Sellers, to join the movement and understood that his own morphing cultural agenda might find sympathy among the city's black residents.

Howard Fuller had been in North Carolina since 1966 serving as chief organizer for the Foundation for Community Development, an offshoot of the North Carolina Fund, which was established in 1963 by Governor Terry Sanford to address poverty. Concurrently, local organizer Nelson Johnson, who enjoyed close ties with many community leaders, had been devising strategies to tackle inequality and discrimination in the schools, housing projects and workplace, William Chafe wrote in *Civilities and Civil Rights*. "By the fall of 1967, Johnson, [activist Tom] Bailey, and Fuller had become convinced that white leaders would respond to black needs only if the entire black community—poor and middle class, high school and college students, average workers and professional people— joined hands to build an independent Black Power base from which to deal with the white community," Chafe wrote. "The key ingredient was to be a coalition between campus and community."

This particular Black Power recipe gave Sellers hope. He liked the idea of combining campus and community to fight injustices in employment and wages, housing and education. By the time he was finished with his master's degree, he was ready for more focused action. Fuller now was working on an ambitious new project, a university start-up that would put the philosophies and goals of Black Power into the classroom in order to train a new generation of African-American nationalists. Though Sellers' legal troubles regarding the Orangeburg Massacre remained unresolved at this time, he embraced the opportunity to help Fuller realize his plan. As if Sellers needed any extra motivation, two more Black Panther friends, Ralph Featherstone and William Herman "Che" Payne, had been killed in a car bomb explosion on March 10, 1970. Featherstone had replaced Sellers as SNCC's program secretary. The two men were in Maryland where Rap Brown was to be tried in connection with an inflammatory speech he had given three years earlier, and they were expected to drive Brown to and from the courthouse. Though authorities had labeled them terrorists, effectively blaming Featherstone and Payne for botching their own bombing attempt, Sellers and many other black activists believed the incident was an assassination, probably one meant to rid the world of Brown.

The need for black empowerment and self-determination seemed more necessary than ever; African Americans were received well by society as entertainers and athletes, and some were entering the political sphere, riding a growing wave of urban discontent in cities that had become majority black, a consequence of white flight. But by and large, the moral force of the heroic phase of the civil rights movement had been overshadowed by reactionary government policies and social attitudes that depended on the vilification of poor black males. Increasingly over the next five decades, young black men—ill-educated, untrained and trapped in poor urban neighborhoods with few prospects for honest work—would bear the brunt of America's domestic corruption. In the South, blacks enjoyed a decade or so of relatively progressive politics, but soon felt the effects of Nixon's Southern Strategy and the resurgence of bigotry, albeit a subtler version of it couched in the rhetoric of liberty, states' rights and heritage.

For Sellers, the ongoing activism in Greensboro, fueled in some measure by Great Society programs such as the Economic Opportunity Act, was a magnet. "I couldn't have landed in a better place," he said. Greensboro's African-American community was fully engaged in efforts to address inequities in the schools, workplace and public housing. Fuller, who wielded a master's degree in social work, had been hired by the Office of Economic Opportunity in Durham and had developed a reputation across the state as an influential community organizer. He had worked closely with Nelson Johnson and others on a variety of projects and direct-action initiatives, including marches in five North Carolina cities to protest the Orangeburg Massacre, an issue near and dear to Sellers' heart. The Durham march on February 16, 1968, had turned violent as hundreds of protestors burned in effigy the figure of South Carolina Governor McNair and scuffled with police. Fire hoses were deployed which scattered the crowd, and Fuller, then 27, had been arrested after intervening in a confrontation between a police officer and protestor.

WHILE TEACHING AT Cornell and studying at Harvard, Sellers was working in 1969 with Fuller, Johnson and other Greensboro activists to set up the Student Organization for Black Unity, or SOBU, a civil rights group meant to support the new generation of black activists in the state and beyond. SOBU gave an official sheen to the campus agitation its members fostered. It was one of dozens of new groups spawned in the late 1960s and early 1970s, as the traditional organizations such as SNCC, SCLC and CORE waned or dissolved. The new wave of organized activism was in many ways the fruit of SNCC's labors, part of its legacy. These groups often included former SNCC members and embraced tactics developed by SNCC. They were often closely aligned with the ideas once propounded by SNCC—those that energized the voter registration drives of the early 1960s and those expressed by the practitioners of Black Power during the late 1960s. What the new crop of civil rights groups shared was a focus on economic

justice. SOBU wanted to facilitate better job training and educational opportunities, for example. Some of the organizations,
such as the New Alliance Party and Progressive Labor Party, were
advocates for workers. Some sought political confrontation; others
were more insular, preferring to strengthen black identity.

Nelson Johnson had arrived in North Carolina in 1965 after
serving in the military and immediately became active in the civil
rights struggle. A student at North Carolina A&T, Johnson got to
know fellow student Jesse Jackson, whom he succeeded as student
body president, and he worked closely with Fuller on efforts to
help poor blacks. Fuller started the Grassroots Association of Poor
People, or GAPP, in 1967 and Johnson ran the Greensboro chapter. The two men became better acquainted with SNCC activists
after the Orangeburg Massacre. Stokely Carmichael, Willie Ricks
and Sellers visited the city in 1968 and helped organize demonstrations. Johnson quickly emerged as Greensboro's main black
leader who was viewed alternately as a helpful negotiator and a
radical intent on social upheaval. "I think we had the most unity
in the African-American community in 1968 and '69 and the early
'70s that I've seen in the 45 years that I've been here," he said in
February 2012. "It was very powerful. It was multi-class. It was
youth, it was poor people, middle-class blacks all working together.
It really was amazing when you think back on it."

Johnson and other activists such as Fuller and Lewis Brandon
soon got to know Sellers well, considering him an experienced
consultant and friend. "He became the spokesman of Black Power
in North Carolina," Johnson said. When it was learned that the
National Student Association, a mostly white liberal group, had
a history of covert support from the CIA, Greensboro's black student leaders severed ties with NSA and organized SOBU, an effort
soon joined by Sellers. "Cleve was kind of an advisor to this newly
developing group," Johnson said.

* ❂ *

BEFORE LONG SOBU would become involved in an incident in Sellers' hometown of Denmark. On April 29, 1969, students at Voorhees College took over an academic building, demanding more black faculty and more black studies from an administration beholden to a white board of trustees and The Episcopal Church with which it was affiliated. Sellers had visited South Carolina the previous week to give a talk at Benedict College in Columbia but had returned to Ithaca, New York, on the weekend before the Voorhees rebellion. Some of the students who occupied the administration building were armed and expected to defend themselves against a militarized police response. South Carolina Governor McNair, determined to avoid another Orangeburg, immediately deployed the National Guard and state troopers to Voorhees, who arrived during productive negotiations between faculty, students and administration, exacerbating tensions. College President John Potts was outraged; a settlement was all but signed. The students were told they had until 3 p.m. to remove themselves; the National Guard sealed the campus, and the school officially shut down at 1 p.m., though hundreds of students remained in the building and in the area. Soon they were forced out. Police made five arrests, and some students were expelled from the school. Potts, who was caught between a white rock and a black hard place, took it personally. He felt betrayed. He had spent many years building up the college, adding dormitories and a cafeteria, augmenting the library, bolstering relationships with supporters, "bending over backwards for the students," according to his daughter Leila Potts-Campbell. In return, students occupied the nerve center of the campus, and the state cracked down hard, against his better judgment. "This is the most devastating thing that ever happened in his whole life," Potts-Campbell said.

SOBU issued a bulletin about the shutdown and armed confrontation. "The circumvention of that peaceful settlement by an
onslaught of armed state forces was a tragedy of immense pro-
portions," SOBU stated. But SOBU had sympathy neither for
Potts nor for the status quo: "It seems so much easier to blame
our failures on a group of frustrated students, a Cleveland Sellers,
a 'creeping socialism,' or any other scapegoats. The public wants
protection from these mythical 'devils' and, unfortunately, there is
little condemnation for the kind of 'protection' which white South
Carolina received in Orangeburg and Denmark."

In some ways, SOBU was the successor to SNCC, though it was
rooted in North Carolina. It was a student group whose members
defended black institutions and promoted an egalitarian ideology
informed by the Black Power movement and Marxist theory, and
they concerned themselves on a day-to-day basis with education,
labor and housing issues. Over the course of about 10 years, SOBU
evolved, just as civil rights groups did previously. Its early emphasis was on pan-African nationalism, but later it would change its
name to Youth Organization for Black Unity (YOBU) and seek
to forge alliances with socialist, labor and liberation groups elsewhere. Its lifespan coincided with the flowering of the black arts
movement and a general assertion of black cultural identity. It also
was operating during a decade of new threats to African-American
communities, Sellers said. "What are the values, and how do we
advance them, especially among people who have become hopeless
and cynical?" And how do you combat Richard Nixon's Southern
Strategy, the demonization of black men, the not-so-subtle racism
of a "law and order" political agenda and the influx of drugs into
the urban ghetto? For Sellers, it was a confusing moment of transition, infused with new threats and persistent hopes.

15 OFF TO PRISON

MEMBERS OF THE nascent SOBU and other organizers, including Sellers, were meeting at North Carolina A&T in May 1969 when students from nearby James B. Dudley High School arrived asking for help. A young man elected president of the student council, Claude Barnes, had been barred from the post without reason by a joint faculty-student election committee. Dudley High was a buttoned-up place, and Barnes was known as a Black Power sympathizer with ties to Nelson Johnson. After a week, on May 21, a high school boycott shifted to the campus of North Carolina A&T and pulled in other community protestors who began throwing bottles and rocks at white motorists. Soon, the young activists

occupied A&T. The situation escalated quickly, with Governor
Robert Scott calling in the National Guard. At 1:30 a.m., gunfire erupted and freshman Willie Ernest Grimes was shot in the
head. He died on the way to the hospital. No one could iden-
tify the shooter, though most blacks in Greensboro believed the
police were to blame. The confrontations continued into the next
day when Guardsmen swept through the campus, breaking down
doors to expel student protestors, many of whom took buses out of
town even as they worried about their grades. Johnson, like Sellers
before him, was identified as the lead agitator. He had insisted
there was no conspiracy and demanded a formal inquiry by the
U.S. Civil Rights Commission, partly to exonerate himself. But
Police Chief Paul Calhoun, testifying before a Senate Investigating
Committee, only cemented in the minds of committee members
the idea that the entire episode was a Black Panther Party plot and
that Johnson had been its chief architect. Calhoun denounced the
black leader as "one of the most militant Negroes in Greensboro."

The North Carolina A&T occupation was not an isolated event.
The university sit-in or building takeover was among the new tactics employed by black activists at the time. On May 3, 1968, students at Northwestern University in Chicago organized a sit-in to
draw attention to low black enrollment. Also in May that year, students at Columbia University occupied Hamilton Hall, protesting
campus racism, the planned construction of a Morningside Park
gymnasium, the Vietnam War and ideological differences between
disaffected black and white students. At Duke, on February 13,
1969, students in the Afro-American Society occupied the Allen
Building (which housed the main administration offices), demanding school reform. In March, students at Howard University took
over the administration building to show solidarity with recently
disciplined colleagues. On April 18, black students at Cornell,
where Sellers was teaching a class on black ideology, took control

of Willard Straight Hall, demanding an end to racist practices and the start of an African-American studies program. (Sellers sympathized with the students, though he said he did not openly advocate militancy or mutiny.) Several more campus takeovers would capture headlines in the months to come.

In Greensboro, Howard Fuller and his colleagues took note of the Allen Building takeover at Duke and, with others, began thinking about creating an experimental college focused on black history and culture. "That was what led to conversations to create Malcolm X Liberation University," he said. "It was at that point I connected with Cleve." MXLU was founded, therefore, in an unsettled atmosphere of renewed activism. To Sellers, it seemed like a very good idea. The school was formed in Durham, North Carolina, opened its doors to students in October 1969, then moved to Greensboro because of that city's larger black community and because an old lodge was made available, with prospects for locating soon on an existing school campus if the property could be secured. Fuller was the driving force, but Sellers played a major role as planner, fundraiser and recruiter of faculty and students. The idea was to provide young blacks with an immersive Africa-centered education that advanced the Black Power cause by transforming African Americans into citizens of the world who, on their own terms, would study African languages and cultures and establish ties with sub-Saharan countries by starting schools, small farms and other enterprises. The school's Curriculum Plan for 1970-71 included an ambitious and unsubtle mission statement that declared the revolutionary intent of MXLU:

> The primary purpose of Malcolm X Liberation University is to provide a framework within which Black education will become relevant to African peoples all over the world and to the struggle for Black liberation. Training will be geared toward

analyzing the political, social, and economic systems and all
institutions of colonizing societies which negatively influence
the thinking of African peoples. The University develops a
Black revolutionary ideology, crystallizes and projects positive
self-awareness, and creates an educational process that builds
and disseminates concepts, techniques, and concrete skills to
the Black community.

Sellers attended all the planning meetings and looked forward to
helping students who had been expelled from other schools because
of their civil rights activism and young people with a social conscience who wanted to investigate questions of identity and join
the fight for justice. "We wanted to draw them to MXLU, teach
them basic courses, trades, agriculture, and talk about the concept of African nationalism and pan-Africanism," he said. Sellers'
experience with SNCC gave him the kind of credentials that students admired, and his international outreach and familiarity with
Africa's post-colonial struggle only reinforced his value to MXLU.
The school's first-year curriculum categories included history
(African civilizations, slavery, colonialism and neo-colonialism);
development of black political thought; language (African tongues
and French); cultural expression; speech; analysis of the colonized
mind; and physical development. The second year would fea-
ture the theme "Nation Building" and include technical training.
Its faculty included James Brewer, a history professor at North
Carolina College; Nathan Garrett, a civic leader; James Graham,
a history professor at Duke; Thomas Rainey, history professor
at Duke; Bunny Small, a Duke graduate with a political science
degree; and Harold Wallace, a Claflin College graduate who stud-
ied education. At the start of the school's first year, the budget
was $80,000, and MXLU had about $12,000 in cash on hand with
monthly expenditures of $9,000. Tuition was $300 a year, but most

of the 51 enrolled students didn't pay it. Grant money came from the Foundation for Community Development in Durham and, thanks to Sellers, The Episcopal Church General Convention Special Program. Sellers expected to remain involved, teaching courses, advising students and collaborating with colleagues. But circumstances soon would get in the way.

ONCE HE FINISHED graduate studies at Harvard in 1970, Sellers could concentrate on Greensboro projects. He also continued to pay visits to college campuses and appeared occasionally before sympathetic audiences to discuss politics, pan-Africanism and, especially, black studies. In 1971 he traveled to Gustavus Adolphus College in St. Peter, Minnesota. While there, he met Gwendolyn Williamson, a student from Memphis, Tennessee, and they hit it off. At first, it was a casual friendship. Sellers was busy in Greensboro, preoccupied with his pending jail sentence, lecturing here and there, uncertain about his future. Gwen Williamson decided to leave Minnesota for Southern Illinois University; she hoped to attend school in New York City, but she was concerned about her parents who were having marital difficulties. "So she decided to come to Greensboro [in 1972] instead to figure things out," Sellers said. Gwen planned to enroll at North Carolina A&T State University. "Come on down," Sellers told her, "but know that I'm working on this Orangeburg thing." In Greensboro, they began to get to know one another.

That fall, Sellers received his jail summons: he was to report in February 1973 to the Goodman Correctional Institution, a few miles up the Broad River from downtown Columbia and adjacent to the headquarters of SLED, the agency most responsible for the Orangeburg Massacre. "But now I've got a little bit of a difficult situation here, because when I get that information, I also get the information that Gwen is pregnant. I don't know what I need to do, but I need to do the honorable thing." He was worried that the authorities would find out about the pregnancy and use it against him, he said. "We had a ceremony in December, and that was a good ceremony. Her parents"—Gwen's father was a minister from Memphis who had been active in the civil rights movement—"were not particularly satisfied but they kind of supported what it was I was trying to do."

What he was trying to do was twofold: defend himself against unfair criminal charges, and draw attention to the Orangeburg Massacre. Many black activists knew about what had happened, but the episode was not widely publicized nor accurately recounted by the news outlets that published stories about it. Most Americans had no idea that the country had experienced its first-ever campus shooting in Orangeburg and that innocent, unarmed students at a historically black college had been killed and injured by state troopers.

"And so in February I went off to prison," Sellers said. Gwen remained in their modest house on Winchester Drive, in the Woodlea neighborhood south of downtown Greensboro. Sellers arranged for two friends, Eric Evans and Thomas Bradley, to look after her and assist her financially. "One guy drove by to check on her. Another guy picked up groceries," Sellers said. "I got [former] SNCC people to raise a little money to help her get by, $20,000-$25,000 for her." She visited her husband every couple of weeks during the seven months that Sellers served. Goodman Correctional Institution Warden Joel T. Wade considered Sellers a political prisoner and a model inmate. "I never saw one more perfect," Wade said. Sellers worked as an assistant clerk, walked six to nine miles a day and tried "to be helpful." He busied himself with reflections on the consequences of civil rights activism, its impact on society and the costs borne by a thousand who agitated for change at the front lines of the battle. He also wrote most of his autobiography, *The River of No Return*, while incarcerated. "He read a lot," Wade said. "Personally I liked the guy. He's a smart man. I had dealings with him every day."

He was in prison until September, grappling with what he knew to be the double affront of being unjustly jailed and missing the birth of his firstborn as a result. One day, he was taken to the prison dentist, located at the Central Correctional Institution, which housed death row. Sellers described it as a dungeon. As he was escorted by six guards down a central aisle traversing a large open room, prisoners lined up on either side, glaring and posturing in a threatening manner. But the way they had arranged themselves, and something about their expression, caused Sellers to realize with a shiver of delight that these men were not angry at all—they were proud of what he had done. It was a show of respect.

WHILE HE WAS serving his time, Sellers learned of the failure in June of Malcolm X Liberation University. The school had fractured into groups of Africanists, who wanted to continue the struggle abroad, and nationalists who wished to confront injustice at home. Fuller had raised the money to buy an old high school, but the Department of Education intervened, instead providing the more established (and less threatening) Bennett College a grant—double the money raised by Fuller—to secure the property. For MXLU administrators already uncertain about the viability of their school, it didn't take much to kill the project entirely. "That was the dagger," Sellers said.

Sellers, who now felt he had merely reached an intermediate station on a long journey, hadn't spent much time considering that he would become old and also didn't believe that he would die a natural death. But he certainly had much to live for, including his wife and his new daughter. Nosizwe Abidemi Sellers was born on May 17, 1973, while Sellers was behind bars. She was named by her godmother, Miriam Makeba. In the Xhosa language, Nosizwe means "mother of the nation"; Abidemi is "born in father's absence" in Yoruba. Nosizwe Sellers would grow up to become a medical doctor.

Marriage proved difficult. The couple struggled with finances, child-rearing obligations and psychological instability, Sellers said. He didn't really get to know Gwen until after prison, and he was discovering he'd married a complicated woman. He was committed to the family, looking for steady work at historically black schools, cooking dinners, taking care of Nosizwe. In January 1975, the family welcomed a son, Cleveland Lumumba Sellers, named in honor of Patrice Lumumba, an anti-colonialist and the first democratically elected leader of the Democratic Republic of the Congo. Cleveland would grow up to become a minister.

Meanwhile, Sellers transformed his lack of steady employment into opportunity, enrolling briefly at Shaw University in Raleigh to finish his undergraduate studies (he majored in education) and obtain his bachelor's degree. Every time he applied for a job, his record—the FBI surveillance, civil rights activities, Orangeburg tragedy—came back to haunt him. He heard about a special two-year North Carolina A&T grant program for social work education that needed a director, and he was appointed to administer it. The grant ended after 18 months, and so did the job. Sellers applied for food stamps. Job applications bore no fruit. He scheduled a series of speaking engagements in an effort to earn enough money to keep the family afloat. In 1976, someone told him about a possible opportunity in the city's personnel office, so Sellers went to meet the woman in charge, Kathleen Soles, a white progressive, well established in Greensboro. His application folder included an FBI report, and Soles told the young job-seeker that the agency had contacted her. Sellers was a provocateur, a militant with a criminal record, the FBI warned. "She became infuriated," Sellers remembered. Soles learned the truth about the South Carolina State shooting and about Sellers' experiences with SNCC, and she was impressed, figuring that Sellers must have good people skills. She gave him a job as interviewer with the City of Greensboro Employment Office. "We developed a tremendous friendship," Sellers said.

Before long, he was promoted to employment director and later took a job in the city's Planning Department administering a job training program made possible by the Comprehensive Employment and Training Act, or CETA, a federal law that took effect at the end of 1973. Sellers was able to employ people as, say, park laborers, low on the totem pole, then watch as they worked their way up, becoming in some cases supervisors. He believed he was rescuing poor men who otherwise might end up in the streets or the gutter or worse and setting them on a proper career path, one that would last decades, pay a living wage and provide a pension.

When he was approached by the press for one reason or another, Sellers—with his boss's approval—spoke openly about his past activism. It was a strategic choice, one that would minimize the chances that the media could "expose" Sellers as a dangerous or disloyal radical. He also cultivated good working relationships with white city employees in the police department, sanitation, parks and recreation, streets and roads and other offices. "I became part of the team," he said.

When Sonja Haynes Stone, an associate professor of Afro-American studies at the University of North Carolina at Chapel Hill, was denied tenure in early 1979, Sellers and most other black activists and academics paid close attention to the ensuing fight and provided moral support. They knew that discriminatory practices made it much more difficult for black professors to qualify for tenure compared to white professors. Stone was respected and beloved at Chapel Hill, but Samuel R. Williamson Jr., dean of the College of Arts and Sciences, did not recommend her for advancement, naming her last day at the school as June 30, 1980. The decision was affirmed a month later along with an intention to phase out the African and African-American studies curriculum. Stone appealed the decision. The NAACP in Durham, the National Council for Black Studies and others, including local activists in nearby cities, came to her defense and, after adjudicated appeals, the UNC board of governors granted her tenure (but not the promotion that usually comes with it).

Sellers had special reason to be concerned about Stone's fate. She had hired him to teach a class in the African-American studies program at UNC-Chapel Hill in the latter part of the 1970s. It was an early, if fleeting, appointment that helped put Sellers on this new academic path. "I had to work out my work schedule at the City of Greensboro, where I went in at 8 a.m. and I got off for lunch at 11. And I would be back by 1:30 p.m. and then I'd work an hour over," he recalled. Stone appreciated Sellers' activist experiences and knew they would enable him to present students with a valuable perspective on black history and the civil rights movement, but she also was acutely aware of academia's professional requirements and counseled Sellers on these demands. "I had to do some work on my resume, getting my curriculum [vitae] all together so it could pass muster," Sellers said. "She said, 'These are things you need to know. I know who you are, but in this organization there are certain criteria that you have to pass. It doesn't serve any purpose to say that you have been in Mississippi and Alabama, you were in Selma, the March on Washington. That's not good enough.'" She wanted him to do the research, to discover the books about Selma and the March on Washington, to publish something himself.

He began to do so, but activist blood ran strong through the veins, and Sellers was eager to introduce students to the ideas that informed the movement and the people who played leading roles. He invited colleagues to deliver guest lectures. One of them was Benjamin Chavis, a member of the Wilmington Ten, who was serving a 34-year sentence in the penitentiary near Raleigh. Later, he would become vice president of the National Council of Churches and, briefly, executive director of the NAACP. But when Chavis was 24 in 1971 and working on behalf of the Commission for Racial Justice to desegregate the public schools in Wilmington, he and nine others were convicted of conspiracy and arson, though Amnesty International and others soon revealed the legal proceedings had been a sham. Sellers wrangled with state bureaucrats to get Chavis out of prison long enough to visit the classroom. "It was tough," Sellers said. Guest lectures by political activists, including those such as Chavis who were paying steep prices for their actions, provided students with unique opportunities to understand the freedom movement and interact with those directly involved. "I had an opportunity to teach some of the sharpest young people in North Carolina at that particular time," Sellers said.

16
GAINING TRACTION
IN GREENSBORO

THE IMPULSE TO CONFRONT injustice and organize his community never left Sellers. During these years in Greensboro, he co-founded Citizens United to Rehabilitate Ex-Offenders. He spearheaded a voter registration drive. He organized a tutoring program to help children improve reading and math skills. He got involved in North Carolina A&T's leadership development program, acting as an advisor to students who respected his background and appreciated his input. He remained as a volunteer after his role in the program was officially over. (The university's 1980 yearbook includes a photograph of school administrators, and there, standing behind the president, even though he held no official post, is Sellers.)

In the fall of 1979, another massacre would take place—this time in Greensboro—and Sellers' response to it would help elevate his stature in the community. On November 3, 1979, the Communist Workers Party, which had been organizing the industrial labor force in Greensboro and counted Nelson Johnson as a member, held a rally and march in opposition to the Ku Klux Klan and the National Socialist Party of America (neo-Nazis). The CWP had been active in campaigning for the rights of black textile workers in the area. The "Death to the Klan" march, co-organized by Johnson, began in the predominantly black Morningside Homes public housing project. Some of the CWP participants were armed and had dared the Klan to attend. Klansmen and Nazis took up the challenge. The Greensboro Police Department had every reason to anticipate trouble: the CWP and Klan had clashed earlier that year; the police department's own paid informant, Klansman Eddie Dawson, had helped orchestrate the confrontation and authorities knew that the Klan planned to bring guns and provoke violence. But the police opted to keep a distance of 20 blocks between themselves and rally participants.

At around 11:20 a.m., a caravan of nine vehicles loaded with Klansmen, their families and neo-Nazis drove into the public housing complex where around 50 protestors had congregated. "From the lead vehicle, Dawson spotted [CWP leader] Paul Bermanzohn, who had invited him to attend the march when they encountered each other at [Nelson] Johnson's press conference at the police department on Nov. 1," according to the Greensboro Truth and Reconciliation Commission Final Report. "Dawson shouted at him, 'You wanted the Klan, you Communist son-of-a-bitch, well you got the Klan!'" The caravan stopped and, before long, Klansmen in the ninth car retrieved guns stowed in the eighth car. Assailants with high-powered weapons shot 13 anti-Klan demonstrators, and killed five of them. A few of the marchers returned fire, but missed their targets. Forty Klansmen and neo-Nazis were involved in the bloodbath, and 16 were arrested; six were tried in the first of two criminal proceedings, and nine were brought to trial the second time. CWP members were not called to testify, and Dawson was never called as a witness. On both occasions, all defendants were acquitted by all-white juries, who cited self-defense and the lack of a racial motive.

Sellers, shaken by yet another mass shooting, organized the public response by calling for the formation of the Progressive Coalition. The NAACP got involved. The Reverend Jesse Jackson responded. The Southern Christian Leadership Conference sent representatives. They planned another rally. They wanted to show the world that the Ku Klux Klan was an evil aberration, that it won no symbolic victory, Sellers said. The city of Greensboro, caught in a tight spot, endorsed Sellers' plans.

Despite resistance from other corners of Greensboro, Sellers helped secure the use of the Greensboro Coliseum, and a huge gathering took place on January 2, 1980. Thousands turned out on a frigid Saturday. CWP members wanted to bring guns. Local police wanted to don helmets and flak jackets. About 300 National Guard troops and 150 state highway patrolmen were deployed to help local law enforcement keep things in check. Sellers argued that Gestapo-like weapons and war paraphernalia would make matters worse. This must be a nonviolent demonstration in which participants keep to the moral high ground, he told them. Stay at the perimeter and let the demonstrators kick and curse if they want to, and if anyone poses a danger, you can bounce them out one at a time, Sellers suggested. The city and its police force went along. Johnson, however, was suspicious of the second rally, accusing Sellers of siding with the enemy. Nevertheless, he participated, along with many of his CWP colleagues and dozens of civil rights organizations. Sharpshooters were strategically positioned in the coliseum. Police organized flyovers. Authorities estimated there were about 3,500 demonstrators, but organizers said there were many more. They were protesting the Klan, to be sure, but they were also commemorating the sit-ins that got their start in Greensboro, labor rights and more. "It was a big success," Sellers said. The people aired their grievances and the tension was diffused.

SELLERS' MONEY PROBLEMS continued. He was living paycheck to paycheck. He hadn't given up on the idea of an academic job, but found his path blocked by his criminal record. In 1983, after Greensboro abandoned an at-large electoral system for city council members in favor of a district system, Sellers decided to throw his hat in the ring. He figured his civil rights activism, city government experience and community organizing skills made him a good candidate. The law forbade city employees from holding public office, so Sellers quit his job and devoted himself fully to his campaign. He solicited letters of support from Mayor Maynard Jackson of Atlanta, Mayor Marion Barry of Washington, D.C. (a SNCC veteran) and Dr. Benjamin Hooks, national president of the NAACP. He came close to securing 50 percent of the votes, narrowing the field of candidates from five to two and prompting a runoff.

His opponent in the runoff, Earl Jones, was a respected black leader who ran an offender rehabilitation program and held a law degree, though he did not practice as an attorney. The election exposed divisions within the black community. Despite a public endorsement of Sellers by Hooks, the scales tipped toward Jones. Black voters had been convinced that Sellers was too militant, tainted by his activist past. Some were warned against voting for him, and a few were harassed at the polls. "This was the only time in my life that I can recall when I really had serious doubts about all of our sacrifices in the movement," Sellers wrote in *The River of No Return*. The loss stung, but the character assassination stung more.

He went back to work for the city of Greensboro, this time as resident resource director of the Housing Authority. He worked with law enforcement to institute community policing programs in public housing projects, among other initiatives. He also dove head first into Jesse Jackson's 1984 presidential campaign, managing activities in North Carolina, South Carolina, Virginia and West Virginia. It was an unexpectedly successful campaign that thrust Jackson into a prominent position on the national stage and sharpened liberal arguments against Ronald Reagan's agenda— Democrats argued that his economic policies favored the rich over the poor, and criticized Reagan's foreign policies that included controversial interventions in Central America and a lack of sympathy for the anti-apartheid cause in South Africa. Jackson also called for a "Rainbow Coalition" of minorities, white liberals, farmers, the poor and working class and the LGBT community. Jackson was only the second African American, after Shirley Chisolm, to run for president, and he was a true contender, winning primaries in Virginia, South Carolina and Louisiana, capturing the District of Columbia and enjoying a very good showing in North Carolina and Mississippi. Jackson also could claim a number of crossover votes and lots of national appeal among progressives. He accumulated nearly 3.3 million primary votes, more than 18 percent of the total.

Sellers joined the campaign because he knew and respected Jackson and because he saw an opportunity to get involved directly in politics as an insider, an organizer and a special advisor—not unlike his friend Ivanhoe Donaldson, a savvy political tactician whom Sellers knew from Freedom Summer and who had run the

New York office of SNCC. Donaldson had assisted Julian Bond with his bid in 1965 for the Georgia House of Representatives, helped Richard Hatcher become mayor of Gary, Indiana, and aided Harold Washington during his 1983 mayoral campaign in Chicago. Donaldson also managed Marion Barry's 1974 campaign for city council in Washington, D.C., and then Barry's upset victory in 1978 that propelled him into the mayor's office. "I was trying to get tied into that," Sellers said of the spate of city-level electoral victories among African Americans. There was another reason he joined forces with Jackson. This was a chance to advance a public agenda first articulated by SNCC and CORE activists in 1964 and interrupted by the Democratic Convention in Atlantic City. It was a way to transform, on a national stage, the self-determination promoted by the Black Power movement into an inclusive strategy that welcomed poor whites and minorities and reordered America's priorities.

Some of Jackson's success was due, in small measure, to Sellers' efforts. "I was responsible for coordination of local campaign organizations, fundraising, primary campaigns, delegate selection, and local conventions in South Carolina, North Carolina, Virginia, and West Virginia," Sellers wrote in his memoir. When it became urgent that the campaign raise $25,000 in 24 hours to secure Jackson a place on the South Carolina primary ballot, Sellers and his colleagues relied on a network of retired school teachers who responded with urgent enthusiasm. In the end, Jackson came in third in the national contest behind Gary Hart and the eventual nominee Walter Mondale. (Four years later, Jackson would run again in the Democratic primary, this time against Michael Dukakis, and do even better, capturing nearly seven million votes and winning 11 contests. Sellers helped in that campaign, too.)

On September 18, 1984, two months after Sellers returned from the Democratic Convention in San Francisco, Gwen Sellers gave birth to a second son, Bakari. The name means "noble promise" or "one who will succeed" in Swahili. Bakari would grow up to become, at 22, the youngest state representative elected to the South Carolina Legislature and a frequent television political commentator.

In the spring of 1987, Sellers received his Ph.D. in education administration from the University of North Carolina at Greensboro. His dissertation was titled "The Civil Rights Movement" and focused on the heroic period between 1954 and 1968. Always interested in the world of higher education, he had secured his key to the doors of academia. Now, he thought, if only the stubborn legal and social barriers could be removed from the entryway. He applied again and again for positions at North Carolina A&T and other HBCUs. Twice he was offered temporary posts funded by grant money, but only thanks to recommendations he received from friends on the faculty. Accepting such short-term jobs would have created more financial and professional instability, not less, so Sellers declined them. Meanwhile, he kept his job with the city's housing authority.

YOUNG PEOPLE IN GREENSBORO were drawn to Cleveland Sellers. They became interested in his story, his mentorship, his attention. He became a surrogate father to Sherman Foust, a poor 12-year-old from the projects who had lost an eye to cancer. Foust was in and out of the Sellers' household frequently, essentially becoming part of the family. Sellers and Gwen made an effort to expose their children to the realities of the world. They visited public housing. The children were taught about thrift, goodwill, charity, public service and humility, and they were shown the results of privilege and reminded of those who had less. "I did that because I didn't want them to develop any kind of attitude," Sellers said.

At the same time, Sellers soft-pedaled the family's financial
uncertainty around his children, who assumed that if the electric-
ity or phone service wasn't working, it was because of a technical problem, not unpaid bills. The kids watched little television
and didn't have cable, according to Nosizwe Sellers. She assumed
the government-subsidized cheese and milk in the house came
from the Housing Authority where her father worked. Sometimes
Sellers would borrow money from his teenaged children, negotiating a favorable interest rate. "Mom hated it because she didn't
want the children to be privy to that part of life," Nosizwe said. But
it felt good to help, to be involved in serious family matters, she
said. In the evenings, the family sometimes would play Monopoly
or other board games. Saturday mornings everyone had assigned
house chores to do. Occasionally, they would go out for dinner,
and the children were expected to show proper etiquette.

"Mom couldn't have chosen a better father for us," Nosizwe
said. "He was very hands-on. It would not be surprising to look
up and see him in the hallways at school. He came to all of our
practices and games"—of which there were many, for Nosizwe ran
track and cross-country, and played softball, basketball and tennis. Other young people in the neighborhood thought of him as a
friendly father figure, sometimes asking him to come to the nearby
park and play basketball. Cleveland Lumumba and Nosizwe
attended summer camps and a tennis academy. Lumumba got in
trouble every time he went fishing because he wasn't allowed to go
alone to the lake. But he would bring back fish to eat. Sometimes
his father would punish him, for one reason or another, using
his belt. The Sellerses kept the back door unlocked; there was
little concern about crime. They employed a housekeeper for
a while named Mira, and when a very young Bakari would call
her "mamma," it irritated his much older sister to no end. Bakari
already had two mothers, she insisted, referring to Gwen Sellers

and herself. In the house, Cleveland Sellers sometimes smoked a pipe. Nosizwe remembers that smell fondly. It signaled that he was home.

But he rarely brought up his tumultuous experiences in the 1960s and early 1970s as a civil rights activist. "As far as the actual activities of the civil rights movement, Daddy didn't really talk about it that much," Nosizwe said. Signs of his commitment, however, often were visible. The family celebrated Kwanzaa each year, and Sellers often hosted special visitors, such as Jesse Jackson, Willie Ricks or Stokely Carmichael in their home. The children thought nothing of it. On one occasion—it was the fall of 1982, when National Football League players went on strike, demanding a 55 percent share of gross revenues—Carmichael was visiting, and Nosizwe, who was nine, took the side of the owners. "Uncle Stokely sat me down to explain I was on the side of the slave masters," she said.

Gwen Sellers sometimes found her husband to be too passive and inscrutable. He was not good at open communication with his wife, not always sensitive to her needs. And Gwen was not always easy to get along with. "I always felt there was tension in the house between my parents, especially with mom," Nosizwe said. "I'm not sure she ever really understood him."

Bakari Sellers remembered sweetened spaghetti for Friday dinners made by his father. "He would add sugar," Bakari recalled with a smile. Cleveland Sellers also prepared fried fish or fried chicken sometimes, with a side of cornbread (with syrup) or grits (with sugar). The family sat together for breakfast and dinner nearly every day. Everyone knew the clearly defined rules. They weren't the rules of an autocrat but, rather, moral guideposts meant to teach values. They often made visits to Denmark to see their grandparents. Bakari remembers their dog Jasper, a big mutt, who would jump the fence and chase anyone nearby. A can next to the stove served as a depository for food scraps, which would be offered to Jasper as a meal, for Jasper ate people food. On Sundays, the children would accompany their grandmother to Bethel AME Church or their grandfather to Rome Baptist Church. The elder pair had remained loyal to their respective church denominations throughout their lives.

By 1989, Pauline and Cleveland Sr. were both in poor health, and their son, exiled in Greensboro for 20 years, decided it was time to come home.

17 PARDONED

TWENTY YEARS AFTER the Orangeburg Massacre, Sellers no longer felt as if he were in the sights of a sniper's gun. Time passes, and with it the passions and anxieties of a particular period. He was ready to assume that South Carolina state troopers probably would not harass him if he returned home. His FBI file had ceased growing by the end of 1971. Most of the left-wing terrorist and Black Nationalist groups spawned by the frustrated activism of the late 1960s had been defeated. It was now the end of the Cold War, and thus the beginning of the end of the government's domestic obsession with so-called communist sympathizers. The Black Power crusade was for the most part relegated to history, partly because many black people were becoming too poor and too over-whelmed by circumstances to maintain a cohesive and influential large-scale movement. During the 1970s President Nixon had declared "war on drugs," and in the 1980s President Reagan made that domestic "war" a priority, introducing mandatory minimum sentencing and forfeiture of property for drug offenses, including non-violent crimes. The new laws disproportionately impacted African Americans. The result was accelerated urban decay and the beginning of the mass incarceration phenomenon.

Sellers had been driving from Greensboro to Denmark every week and was eager to find a job and a place to live in the area. His parents were coping with worsening maladies—his father's prostate cancer had metastasized, and his mother's cancer had returned (she had had a double mastectomy five years earlier). He needed to drive his mother to Columbia Hospital for chemother-apy. It seemed the tables had turned: now it was Cleve Sellers who was worried about his parents. For two years he strategized from Greensboro about returning to South Carolina. Then in February 1990 Cleveland Sellers Sr. died. Not long after, Sellers was on the way to see his mother and stopped six miles up the road to watch a basketball game between the Denmark and Blackville high school teams. When he arrived at her house three hours later than expected, he discovered that his mother had called the police. "I just did not know where you were," she explained. Her concern for her son's safety had not diminished. Twenty-five years later, Sellers remembered the episode with regret.

He had a tendency to inject a degree of optimism into the topic of his mother's illness, but one day he was forced to confront the reality of her condition. She lifted her shirt to show him a chest deformed by surgery and discolored by the spreading cancer. If shock was intended, it worked. "I had to sit down," Sellers recalled. She told her son she was reconciled with death, that there was no good reason for her to continue suffering. Her husband now was gone. "I think she was living to take care of him," Sellers said. He moved into his mother's house in August 1990, intending to settle in and find a good job before his wife and children joined him that December. Pauline Taggert Sellers passed away that fall.

Sellers knew he could rely on a little rental income from tenants living in his father's properties. He submitted applications to the state's HBCUs, which cluster in the Midlands, but his criminal record got in the way. He landed a short-term adjunct position at Denmark Technical College in the first part of 1991, teaching sociology and social work. He was trying to gain his footing in his home state and slowly making progress. The next year, he was appointed by local officials to the South Carolina State Board of Education, representing the second judicial district, which included Bamberg County. Promptly he got to work advocating for new programs meant to help low-income children living in rural areas where education rarely consisted of more than the basics, and where the basics often were not up to snuff. He wanted young black students to build up their self-esteem through academic accomplishment. He pushed for reforms that would help, especially, young black males who were most at risk for enduring lives of poverty, crime and hopelessness. He helped start little league football and soccer; he worked to reopen a recreation center. Securing a seat on the board was a small turning point: it gave Sellers a public profile in his home state. He sensed that the curse of Orangeburg soon could be lifted, though he knew not how.

AT THE END OF 1992, the subject of Sellers came up in a conversation between writer Jack Bass, co-author of *The Orangeburg Massacre*, and a friend. Bass, who published his book in 1970, was living and working in Oxford, Mississippi, at the time. "Why doesn't the governor pardon Sellers?" the friend wanted to know. In South Carolina, it turned out, pardons are issued not by the governor but by the Probation, Pardon and Parole Board. A short while later, Bass ran into Rhett Jackson, a Columbia bookseller, civil rights advocate and one-time member of the Department of Probation, Pardon and Parole Services. Jackson's wife and Bass's sister had been classmates in high school.

"How does somebody get a pardon?" Bass asked.

"You have to apply for it," Jackson replied.

It was as simple as that. Bass stopped at Hilton Head Island for a Christmas vacation with his wife. She wanted to visit relatives in Denmark, so the couple went there and Bass looked up Sellers in the phone book. Together, they prepared the application and gathered letters of recommendation from the sheriff of Bamberg County, the Greensboro police chief and others. Several months later, Bass was in Columbia attending a trial. "I called up Rhett Jackson just for the hell of it," he said. "[The board] had just decided to grant the pardon, that morning or the previous day." It was Tuesday, July 20, 1993. News cameras were sent to the Board of Education meeting Sellers was attending. That Sunday, The State newspaper in Columbia published a strongly supportive editorial stating that the pardon "was long, long overdue" and "a significant step toward reconciliation and the healing process."

Sellers told the Orangeburg Times and Democrat that he was elated by the pardon. "It closes a chapter in my life; it lifts the burden of proof from my shoulders in reference to what took place in Orangeburg. This pardon says I was not guilty of any wrongdoing...and it gives me an opportunity to pursue work in higher education." He told the reporter that his next step was clear: "I plan to seek to have the conviction expunged from my record," Sellers said. Under South Carolina law, a pardon neutralizes but does not remove criminal convictions. To this day, Sellers' riot conviction remains in place. He has shed any concern about it, though, and considers it a badge of honor.

Looking back on that moment in 1993, Sellers said the pardon unfortunately was not akin to an admission of error; it was merely an indication of a significant shift in the way he was perceived by political and civic leaders in the state. Nevertheless, after 25 years of a kind of purgatory, he was relieved, happy and grateful for the support he received from colleagues and acquaintances who vouched for him. Sellers' pardon in 1993 initiated a lasting friendship with Bass, who has never stopped reminding those willing to listen about the Orangeburg Massacre's corrosive impact on its victims and on the state, and who has consistently defended his friend.

GOVERNOR ROBERT MCNAIR, though, was less inclined to acknowledge that Sellers was not the provocateur. McNair held tightly to the notion that the SNCC activist was behind the violence of February 8, 1968. "I still think that had Cleveland Sellers not precipitated a confrontation, nor forced a confrontation, that the thing would have calmed down, and we would have resolved it," he said in an oral history recording. "If there was any one person that was really responsible for the deaths of these three kids down there, it was Cleveland Sellers, more than anyone else, because they wouldn't have been there had it not been for him.... So when you come to the bottom line, he incited the riot."

In 1996, Sellers struck up a correspondence with McNair, writing a letter encouraging the former governor to "bring closure to the Orangeburg Massacre" and "clean the slate" by issuing an apology and implementing some kind of truth and reconciliation process. He wrote again in 2000 to explain how the Orangeburg crisis had compromised his ability to find remunerable work.

Sellers wrote again in 2001, this time sending McNair an impassioned two-page plea for understanding and accord. "What could have been my motive?" Sellers asked, referring to the former governor's stubborn insistence that the activist was responsible for the deadly campus confrontation. He continued:

> While I may not be given credit for being brilliant, my extensive experience in Alabama and Mississippi with terror, violence, brutal police and racial zealots would be sufficient experiences for me not to be stupid. Why would anyone have black students, unarmed and at night, charge armed white police? It does not make sense to me now and it did not make sense to me in 1968. I was the 'scapegoat'...someone to hide the truth behind. My goal was for people to empower themselves and take control of their lives and to *live* as human beings—fighting the racial prejudice and discrimination that in 1968 permeated South Carolina. I was *never* interested in desegregating a bowling alley.

McNair went to his grave in 2007 unconvinced by Sellers' arguments.

SOON AFTER THE PARDON, Sellers came to the attention of officials at the University of South Carolina, who were nurturing an African-American studies program. The activist who grew up in Denmark, who marched throughout the South, who raised his fist in solidarity with Black Power advocates, who was shot in Orangeburg, tried and jailed, who rallied laborers and protesters after the Greensboro anti-Klan rally—the man who had experienced so much as a warrior at the front lines of the battle—was granted an appointment as a visiting professor at USC. Finally, at nearly 50, he was going to be a full-fledged academic. Finally, he could impart from within the establishment the hard lessons of civil rights and convey how justice is not only an ideal but a physical requirement. Sellers always had been a teacher. Now, he was going to be full-time faculty.

18

WITHIN THE ESTABLISHMENT

THE UNIVERSITY OF SOUTH CAROLINA is among institutions that comprise what we think of as "the establishment." Chartered in 1801, the university in downtown Columbia offers some 350 degree programs, training people to become active participants in the intellectual, cultural, economic and political pursuits of their communities. Into this establishment walked Dr. Cleveland Louis Sellers Jr., 38 years after Emmett Till was slain in Mississippi, 33 years after the Greensboro sit-ins, 25 years after the campus shootings at South Carolina State College in Orangeburg. Joining this establishment in 1993 was a man who for years was marginalized, *anti-establishment*, a man who had been vilified by white society, a man who fought the status quo, who worked toward a day when people might join together in common purpose. To Sellers, the civil rights struggle had always been about equal participation and changing society from within, not wholesale revolution. Now, in a culmination of sorts, Sellers was reaping some of the fruits of this accomplishment, though he knew there was much left to do. These external goals, whose targets were students and society, were just half the battle. Within academia, the challenge of nurturing a reputable program was the other half.

Much later, USC President Harris Pastides would say that the African-American studies program grew to become "part of the fabric" of the campus, helping to draw a diverse faculty and student body, adding both academic and social value to the community, and aiding in retention efforts. "There is no doubt in my mind that that program is here to stay. That is Cleveland Sellers' legacy." That legacy didn't transpire easily or quickly. Sellers got his start as a member of the history department, serving as assistant director of the African-American studies program, which had begun in 1971.

Jon Michael Spencer, a musicologist, was in charge when Sellers arrived, but the program was struggling under his leadership. He was the fifth full-time director in 22 years, following Willie Harris, Grace McFadden and Jim Miller, with two interim directors in between. Spencer left the post after about a year. Scholar Andrew Billingsley, whom Sellers had helped hire, suggested that the school make Sellers interim director while the department considered launching a new outside search. But that new search never transpired; Sellers, who received tutelage from his history colleague Walter Edgar, was deemed worthy of the position and quickly made it his own, adopting a student-focused approach. By becoming an administrator, Sellers was able to cement his position at the university while avoiding tenure requirements, he said. He was an activist-turned-academic, ensconced in the history department and tasked with bolstering the sort of cultural studies program that has long been (and remains still today) under fire on some college campuses. Black studies, Jewish studies, Caribbean studies, women's studies, LGBT studies—these are areas of scholarship that don't fit neatly into traditional academic categories. They focus, in large measure, on issues that are unfolding before our eyes. The need for such programs is obvious to many: they provide safe havens in which young people can feel empowered to examine and question the world in which they live and the many factors that contribute to the formation of "history." Such programs also allow them to apply to their lives what they discover through intellectual exercise. This is often why some students gravitate to cultural studies in the first place, and this is why activist-teachers like Sellers have found this corner of academia so appealing: they can share their own experiences and lessons learned.

But it is also why such teachers sometimes don't fit neatly into academia's prescribed stations. Higher education has its rules for historians and other scholars: a Ph.D. is required, as are research, published articles and books, conference participation and more. But the strengths brought to the job by a former political activist and agitator are not always the same as the strengths brought by someone who has prioritized libraries over liberation. Sellers had earned a Ph.D. in education, not history, yet ended up part of the University of South Carolina's history department. "So that's where the tension was," said Valinda Littlefield, director of African-American studies at the school. "It eased though, and Cleve garnered a lot of respect." He expanded the program, recruiting students and academic allies from various departments, then began to hire faculty with support from a university intent on educating young people in a state whose history is intrinsically wound up with slavery and oppression.

Among those Sellers hired was Patricia Sullivan, a professor at Harvard University's W.E.B. Du Bois Institute and author of *Lift Every Voice: The NAACP and the Making of the Civil Rights Movement*, and Kent Germany, who transferred from the University of Virginia in 2006, in large measure to work directly with Sellers on a civil rights oral history project. The two men discussed not just this effort to document the voices of South Carolina activists, but "a broader project," part two of *River of No Return*, a biographical history of Sellers' life after 1969, Germany said. (The project was never completed.) Others in South Carolina have pursued the civil rights oral history initiative, including Bobby Donaldson at the university and the United Methodist minister Marvin Lare.

"He was a good guy to work with," Germany said, recalling the time he and Sellers spent together at USC. "You can see why he was such an effective organizer, because he doesn't tell you what you should think. The meetings that he would run were not run like Cleveland was in charge of everything and this is how we were going to do it. He was very much somebody who got feedback from everybody and walked us through, and then you would arrive probably where he wanted you to go in the first place." This method surely was developed during his years with SNCC, Germany added. Under Sellers' leadership, the African-American studies program at USC became a model in its field of the interdisciplinary approach that borrows faculty from various departments such as history and political science. It started small, with little money and equivocal support, causing directors to come and go over the years, partly because of funding concerns, Germany said. "Cleve offered stability."

As often happens to civil rights leaders after years of activism, Sellers encountered on this neutral territory a former enemy, Carl B. Stokes, head of security at USC during the years Sellers ran the African-American studies program. Stokes was among the troopers involved in the Orangeburg Massacre. He was one of SLED Chief J.P. Strom's assistants on the scene. Once or twice, the two men bumped into one another on campus. "He has changed," Stokes was reported to say of Sellers.

Although he brought years of experience as a prominent civil rights activist to the job, Sellers never really played that card as an academic administrator seeking to assert his authority. Rather, Germany said, he exhibited humility and openness, welcoming a variety of political and historical arguments regardless of the ideologies and experiences that informed those views. "There was, I think, a genius to it," Germany said. "I think he was very careful about appearing to be confrontational. I think he shied away from being 'that radical' at the university, I think because so many people were expecting that.... He's really guarded about using his history as a weapon." The result was that students, and Sellers' own colleagues, gained a nuanced understanding of the civil rights movement, an appreciation for the many lesser-known figures, black and white, who dedicated themselves to the fight for freedom and enfranchisement. Because of Sellers' knowledge of the minutiae of civil rights history, "my understanding is far different than the grand narrative," Germany said.

Valinda Littlefield first met Sellers in 1999 when she arrived at the University of South Carolina. He was then associate director for curriculum. Her first impression was positive: "He was handsome, very engaging, very nice, a little quiet in a way," she said. "He has to warm up to you." Sellers' success in the program coincided with a push for diaspora studies, Littlefield said. The program started to open up a bit, to focus increasingly not just on the African-American experience but on current events and their impacts, on foreign policy and its effects on black people around the world, on migration within the broader African diaspora and on democracy itself. In addition to research on health and wealth

disparities, environmental inequities and other contemporary concerns, there is still much to uncover about the civil rights movement itself, a movement that spawned black studies programs in
the first place and provided those programs with some of their
first scholars, Littlefield noted. These are the challenges faced by
scholars who specialize in the sometimes enigmatic discipline of
"cultural studies." Those challenges now are being confronted by
professors whose footings have been made more secure thanks to
the solid foundation Sellers helped build, and thanks to his insistence on putting students first, Littlefield said. "He was never, ever
too busy to talk to a student," she said. "You don't often see people
who will take that kind of time, or who have that kind of time to
take. You do lose something in the process, but he was very ada-
mant about reaching that next generation. That was his legacy."

THE STUDENTS WERE most important, of course, but Sellers,
as always, saw the bigger picture. He understood that his position
lent him influence, and not just on campus. "We were using the
program as a way to reach out to the community, and we were also
engaged in trying to increase the numbers of minority professors
and students," Sellers said. "So during that time that I was in the
African-American Studies program, …you will find that the per-
centage of African-American students increased substantially.…I
think we got up to where the school was actually 19 percent African
Americans. That includes graduate and undergraduate." He also
was interested in emphasizing the historical significance of the
Orangeburg Massacre, which he considered a litmus test for South
Carolina. If the episode could not be addressed with honesty, if
a formal state-backed investigation was never to be undertaken,
if residents of the state knew little of this watershed moment, if
whites persisted in dismissing the concerns of blacks who viewed

the shooting as a pronounced symptom of South Carolina's racial discord, then no grand "truth and reconciliation" achievement was possible. So he encouraged his students to do research and write papers on the Orangeburg Massacre. In so doing, they interviewed many state actors, asked important questions and ensured the topic remained vital.

During his years in Columbia, Sellers met and mentored another young person who had lost his way. Jodie Walker was a student at the College of Charleston who transferred to USC after a knee injury, Sellers said. "He was there in Columbia, but he just couldn't seem to get his direction together, you know? He was disappointed that he was no longer an athlete....He just didn't have anybody to go to and be a sounding board or somebody who took an interest in him as a person. And so I took an interest in him and he got to meet Bakari and Nosizwe and Lumumba and all." Sellers became a surrogate father of sorts, taking Walker with him to meetings and events. "We got him through the University of South Carolina, we got him into a master's program," Sellers said. Eventually, Walker relocated to Spartanburg, married and started a family. "But Jodie is somebody who is always around. He's right at the end of the family, all the kids know him and, you know, they all reach out to each other, they all help each other. They all talk to each other still on a regular basis."

CULTURAL STUDIES PROGRAMS like the one Sellers ran require special handling, said Andrew A. Sorensen, who served as USC president from 2002 to 2008. If you create unique departments, you run the risk of "ghettoizing" them. They must be part of the school's larger mission. What's more, Sorensen said, cultural studies programs are of little use if they do not draw resources from the broader community. Within a week of his appointment to the presidency, Sorensen was told by several people that there was a gulf between the university and Columbia's black community. So he set up an African-American Advisory Board to engage leaders and improve school programming. "Word spread like wildfire," he said. As a young man, Sorensen had worked as a volunteer for the Southern Christian Leadership Conference.

Sorensen, a white man, said a history of activism was widely considered an asset in academic circles. "If you were an African American and an activist in the cause, that counted for something." It was expected that senior administrators in African-American studies programs would advocate scholarship *and* action. But developing such programs was not easy. Anxious white administrators often worried that stirring the pot of black history would provoke unrest among black students and whites sympathetic with their concerns. Sorensen said Sellers was ideal for the academic world: a "very gentle person" who possessed "terrifically strong convictions" and a willingness to balance scholarship with service.

When activists—who may or may not pursue scholarly projects in the standard manner—assume academic positions at a university, some strain occasionally emerges between them and traditional faculty members. "It's been an issue in Cleveland's career," Germany noted. "He didn't fit neatly into a place that would put him on a tenure track. [So] there's definitely tension, even though more people read his book than all other books [by his colleagues] combined....To accommodate somebody whose status and stature comes from what they do outside of the academy, it creates problems in the academy because the academy doesn't quite know what to do with people like that."

This problem is much diminished at most HBCUs whose fundamental *raison d'etre* is to make higher education more accessible to as many black students (especially low-income black students) as possible. HBCUs can help bridge an economic gap. So in June

2008 when Sellers was invited to assume the post of president at Voorhees College in his hometown of Denmark, he didn't have to think about it for long. Here was an opportunity to ascend to a coveted position, to lead a school that, in its earlier segregation-era iteration, had educated and nurtured him; here was a chance to put to use some of the lessons learned and skills developed during his years of civil rights activism. Throughout his career he had sought to introduce and codify black studies on college campuses, both predominantly white and predominantly black. This was a legacy of the Black Power movement. Sellers had advocated for a greater appreciation of African-American history, culture and identity on every campus he crossed: Howard, Cornell, Harvard, the University of North Carolina, Malcolm X Liberation University, the University of South Carolina. Now his career would reach its culmination at Voorhees. This was a direct extension of his life-long civil rights work and the full realization of a key aspect of SNCC's agenda: to educate young black people and instill in them a sense of self-worth and pride.

Fifteen years earlier, Sellers had struggled to find a decent teaching job, hindered by his criminal record and late to the game because of a self-imposed 20-year exile in Greensboro. Now he was a college president.

19 CLOSING THE CIRCLE

IN JUNE 2008, Cleveland Sellers Jr. was appointed to serve as the eighth president of Voorhees College. As a student of Voorhees High School, Sellers had heard civil rights lectures in those same buildings. He had worshipped at St. Philip's Chapel, the Episcopal parish on campus where he served as a young acolyte, following the lead of his beloved activist priest. In accepting the presidency of this 111-year-old historically black college, Sellers closed the circle. And he felt somewhat vindicated, for he had served on the school's board of trustees in the 1990s and had been dismissed after contesting plans to tear down an historic building on campus. He also had raised concerns on the board about payroll irregularities and possible nepotism. "Becoming president was a little like [the board] making amends," he said. Sellers replaced Dr. Lee Everett Monroe Jr., who served three and a half years but resigned when a civil jury in U.S. District Court in Columbia concluded that he was guilty of sexual harassment against a female professor.

Cleve and Gwen Sellers occupied the president's house, a comfortable residence on campus, tucked among a grove of pine trees. Gwen was happy to live in a rural place with quick access to nature and to gardens where she could "play in the dirt," she recalled. While her hometown of Memphis, Tennessee, had offered a certain cosmopolitan atmosphere, and her years in Greensboro were enhanced by urban amenities, life in quiet Denmark was a big change. She had to make her own fun, she said.

Carrie Simmons was the 74-year-old mayor of Denmark in 2008, and she put great hopes in Sellers when he took the helm of Voorhees. The college provided more jobs than any other employer in the area (about 400) and was meant to function as an economic engine, turning out the next generation of educated professionals. Simmons had tried to improve the town. Before Sellers' arrival, a park had been named for local artist Jim Harrison. The city renovated the Dane Theater, and the fire department got a new building. Her plans included more parks, a farmers' market and the recruitment of small businesses and retail stores. Most importantly, she wanted to forge a long-term working relationship with Voorhees College, one that might result in the formation of a community development corporation whose goal was to make affordable housing available to residents and provide them with a venue for special performances and events. Simmons had known the Sellers family for a long time. She believed a city-college partnership could get Denmark back on its feet. "Voorhees is key," she said. "The college always has been interchangeable with the city."

But such advances were hard to achieve. Denmark was a rural

community long neglected by South Carolina's political operatives and abandoned by many of its young sons and daughters who, if they expected to flourish in the wider world, were forced to seek their fortunes elsewhere. This was still the case as Sellers assumed the helm of Voorhees. Denmark was a tiny town, one of scores in the state whose remaining residents often relied on nostalgia-fueled memories to picture a more vibrant community. And nothing about current social and economic trends indicated that such communities would regain any of their former vitality.

ENROLLMENT AT VOORHEES had slipped from about 800 a few years before Sellers arrived to fewer than 600 when he assumed the presidency. Like many historically black college and universities, Voorhees faced financial, enrollment and academic challenges in 2008. HBCUs—roughly 100 of them in the United States—had been founded to provide higher education to African Americans locked out of a traditional college setting because of segregation. But as integration rolled through the South in the 1970s and onward, competition for talented students became fierce. Major colleges around the country aggressively recruited gifted black students as they sought to diversify their student populations. Bolstered by their impressive scholarship endowments, major universities whisked away many of the most talented students. In-state colleges recognized their student populations were overly white and recruited high-achieving black students, too. Not only that, but Voorhees faced competition for students with six other HBCUs in the state—Allen University and Benedict College in Columbia; Claflin University in nearby Orangeburg; Clinton College in Rock Hill; and Morris College in Sumter.

Among Sellers' first actions as president was the announcement of a five-year goal to double enrollment. Sellers intended to reach beyond Bamberg and Orangeburg counties into neighboring rural areas, and well into the Lowcountry, in order to achieve it. He sought to diversify the student body by inviting students from the Caribbean, South America and Africa to participate in a "community of learning," and in so doing, to instill in Voorhees students a global perspective, he said. He also hoped to develop the liberal arts curriculum, strengthen science education and attract new faculty. Some of the buildings on the college's 345-acre campus needed renovation. The athletic program needed improvement. Early on, he believed that Voorhees needed a football team. Without football, Voorhees could not qualify for a college conference. With football, the college could become more attractive to students and investors. (Introducing football would prove too expensive and impractical, and Sellers quickly gave up on the idea.)

At the start of his term at Voorhees, the school's slogan was "Tempered by the past, poised for the future." LaTonya Gillespie, a senior biology major at Voorhees when the new president took the reins, noted in a 2008 that students had much to learn from Sellers and his career as an activist. He could teach lessons of empowerment, inspire students to overcome obstacles and share with them the importance of commitment, "because it's harder than ever to succeed," Gillespie said. So Sellers did what he could. He hit the road to help with recruitment; he met with Episcopal Church officials and many others in an attempt to secure private funding; he researched what it would take to bolster the college's athletics program; he worked on staffing improvements and infrastructure upgrades and he did his part to stimulate students with his grand ideas of identity and history. He invited poet and SNCC alumna Nikki Giovanni to campus, as well as Jesse Jackson and other prominent black leaders and artists. He believed strongly that a college education was about much more than mastering core subjects and preparing for a career.

* ❁ *

EIGHT YEARS INTO Sellers' tenure, total enrollment at Voorhees hovered a little above 600, a slight improvement but nowhere near his five-year goal of 1,200. The campus remained largely unchanged, as did the funding and faculty recruitment challenges. At about $20,000 a year for tuition, and on-campus housing, Voorhees was a relatively economical alternative to bigger, more prestigious schools like Clemson or the College of Charleston, but its costs were nearly identical to those at, say, Coastal Carolina University in Conway and just $7,000 less than costs at Winthrop University in Rock Hill.

While some HBCUs, such as Morehouse, Howard, Spelman, Tuskegee and Xavier managed to carry on successfully in a post-segregation environment, others faced obstacles that sometimes seemed insurmountable. Walter E. Massey, president of Morehouse College, articulated the problem in a 2006 essay:

> Generally, historically black colleges and universities face the same challenges that most other colleges and universities face, and those include maintaining academic excellence, competing for the best students, and building a sound and stable financial base. In addition to these challenges, HBCUs face the additional challenge of preserving the best features of their heritage and mission, while not becoming mired in the past. Historically black institutions cannot assume that their tradition, historic heritage, and mission will allow them to be successful in the future. They must be willing to adapt to the changing environment of higher education in the 21st century.

Sellers recognized that colleges like Voorhees were no longer the only options for African-American students seeking to advance their learning. Their purpose had to change. Sellers saw it this way:

They would educate, in large measure, the underserved and marginalized, students whose families couldn't afford the costs of state universities. But there were challenges and obstacles, and HBCUs were pressured to conform to the rules, habits and preferences of a predominantly white society. They must be accredited. They must take into account standardized test scores. They must cultivate donors. The biggest donor base for colleges and universities is their pool of alumni. But alumni of black schools like Voorhees are generally not as wealthy as their white counterparts, and they have less inherited money, so naturally they give less. Institutionalized disadvantage impacts African Americans broadly and could be observed in microcosm at Voorhees and other HBCUs.

In 2010, Sellers established an endowment for Voorhees in the name of his parents, the largest by any alumnus. By 2018, the fund had about $55,000 in it. The school benefited from a couple of smaller personal endowments set up by others. The invested funds did not generate significant interest income the school could use to fund capital projects, faculty or programming. Declines in student enrollment over the years had resulted in lost revenue and increased financial hardship at Voorhees. "We can't stand any reduction in revenue," Sellers told the Episcopal News Service as he neared the end of his service at the school. "We're already on the margin in many instances." And with little help from the endowment, "we don't have any kind of way to make up for our students who are not here."

The recession of 2008 hit Voorhees hard. The school no longer could provide about 100 modest scholarships to its students, though Sellers succeeded in regaining that small financial leverage in the years that followed, he said. When Congress passed the Consolidated Appropriations Act of 2012, it radically changed eligibility requirements for federal Pell Grant applicants, and this, too, was a blow to Voorhees. The changes, which disproportionately impacted minority students, reduced the number of semesters students could receive a full-time Pell Grant; forced more low-income families to contribute to the cost of their children's education; reduced the number of eligible grant recipients; and required students to pass an "ability to benefit" test. The year before the loan policy changed, Voorhees had about 270 students who received a federal grant. After the change, many of these students no longer were eligible. Some were forced to find jobs, Sellers said. "A lot of students had to drop out because of financial strain." Sellers recognized that many Voorhees students struggle with poverty and cope with significant emotional and psychological issues. "Others come and appreciate the bed and meal plan," for the school environment can be more stable, more reliable than home, Sellers said. Occasionally he encountered a student who could not afford to use the laundry machines, so he would surreptitiously hand over two dollars in coins.

For Sellers, the uphill push was constant, he said. Nevertheless, Voorhees adhered to a mission shared by many similar schools. Consider the goals laid out by Xavier University President Norman C. Francis, who said that although black colleges in the 21st century are obligated to offer a quality education to all, "our institutional missions remain...especially supportive of African Americans, who need both an affirmative caring system and access to the quality education we offer. As long as the playing field is not equal, we are obligated to make sure that the access and opportunity for higher education is available for African Americans....We must continue to emphasize the heritage aspect of the mission. There is no reason not to, and particularly when we are open to anyone who wishes to come to receive the quality of education we offer."

For smaller private HBCUs like Voorhees, these goals certainly are shared, but achieving them can be very difficult, for such schools often serve students who are not college-ready because of

faulty primary and secondary education systems and the deleteri-
ous effects of poverty. A goal might be to provide a path to the professional class for success-minded young people, but when those
young people struggle with basic writing, math and science skills,
the path is full of obstacles, curves and dead-ends. But African-
American civic leaders like Sellers are accustomed to navigating a
winding road strewn with obstacles; they know that for every two
steps forward one often takes a step back; they remain determined
to ensure access to the path, no matter its condition. A difficult
path to tread is better than no path at all.

Sellers said it helps when an HBCU leader has prior experience with such institutions, clear goals, fundraising expertise and
a determination to bolster and uphold the integrity of the school.
"Sometimes people choose not to do the right things," he said. "We
need to have principled people in these positions, and have young
people in these positions who can travel and find resources.... You
can't have a stable school if you have turnover every two years in
the top office." An HBCU must cultivate a brand, encourage its
students to "tell their stories, how school changed their lives," he
said. And boards of directors must be populated with credentialed
people who can reconcile high expectations with institutional and
educational realities.

Leading Voorhees forced Sellers to navigate a rocky road, but
it also helped fuel a basic impulse to stand up for under-privileged
African Americans. "I wouldn't change it for any experience I've
had," he said. Under Sellers, the college upgraded its computer system, installed Wi-Fi throughout campus, made classroom assignments available online, strengthened its focus on the sciences,
improved its cybersecurity protocols and created internship opportunities for students. "I had hoped to do the entire 10 years," Sellers
said. "But a lot came to fruition. It's about incremental improvements. I'm satisfied with my eight years there. I did all I could do."

20 INHERITANCE

BACK IN DENMARK, Sellers' life changed radically. His children were grown and gone; his relationship with his wife Gwen, always challenging, often strained, was becoming untenable. They had access to both the president's house on campus, a large and comfortable residence, and to their own home they had purchased, just up the street, but Sellers was more isolated than he had been in Columbia, Greensboro or Atlanta. He traveled farther afield to attend conferences, convene with old civil rights movement colleagues, deliver a speech here or there. But mostly his life was now centered in this tiny rural town.

One effect of integration on Denmark and other small southern towns was the onset of a long economic decline, especially within

black communities. Many left their rural surroundings for opportunities in bigger cities or at factories some distance from home.
In the NAFTA era, manufacturing companies began relocating
their plants to Mexico and countries overseas, drying up employment opportunities in places like the Black Belt of South Carolina.
What's more, the old roads linking urban centers and running
through places such as Denmark, which had benefited from the
traffic of travelers and businessmen, were replaced with interstate
highways that bypassed small towns. Once-segregated schools
became desegregated but still were populated by all blacks or all
whites. The poor residents of Denmark became poorer, bereft of
an independent black economy.

As president of Voorhees, Sellers was the biggest fish in the
pond, and he maintained after all those years a sense of obligation
to the community, an obligation freely, even joyfully, expressed.
His commitment reached well beyond the boundaries of the
campus. He looked in on people, especially the dispossessed; he
brought them groceries. He stopped to chat with residents at the
store or standing on a street corner. As he drove through Denmark
in his comfortable Buick, townsfolk waved at a man they considered a prodigal son, a man who had achieved something, who had
seen the world but who had not forgotten his origins.

Then, suddenly, problems. First it was his marriage. He had
long struggled, and mostly failed, to sustain a certain equilibrium
in his relationship with Gwen and between his family commitment and his public life, he admitted. Gwen was diagnosed with
chronic myeloid leukemia in 2014. Treatment proved successful,
but the ordeal took its toll on an already tense and faltering marriage. Sellers visited his friend Jack Bass in Charleston with one
excuse or another, but mostly to get away from home for a brief
spell. Soon the marriage was over. Sellers remained in the president's house on the Voorhees campus. Gwen Sellers relocated to

Columbia to be closer to her son Bakari, her daughter Nosizwe and reliable medical services.

In 2015, the second shoe dropped. Sellers endured a health crisis of his own that nearly killed him. A weakened heart began to give out, at first causing fatigue but soon prompting a crisis. He was rushed to Duke University Hospital in North Carolina, which is known for its excellent cardiac doctors and progressive treatment discipline. He endured many tests as the medical team fretted about a heart that was functioning at merely 20 percent of its capacity. The children were worried. Friends and colleagues held their breath. The people who comprised Sellers' inner circle prepared themselves for the worst. Within a few months, his condition stabilized, but his doctors warned him against excessive physical and mental exertion. They recommended that he retire from his post at Voorhees College.

Reluctantly (for there was still so much left to do), Sellers obliged. On Thursday, September 17, 2015, a 70-year-old Sellers took the podium outside the administrative offices on campus and, with emotion swelling in his voice, announced he would step down as president at the end of that academic year. "Serious health challenges make this decision necessary at this time," he said. "This decision does not come lightly. The Voorhees College family has become my own. The ties that bind me to this prestigious institution are that I am an alum, but also go far beyond my years on this Earth, to the time of my parents and the connection we hold with Denmark, South Carolina. My support will never diminish and I will always be a Voorhees Tiger in mind, body and spirit."

Always a Voorhees Tiger. It sounds trite to say that Sellers had come full circle, perhaps because that implies a life lived with a sense of destiny, a life neatly tied at its two ends. Cleveland Sellers Jr. did not live his life neatly, and he did not always know what trajectory it would take. He was not fated to join the civil rights movement or to attach himself to Stokely Carmichael or to embrace the Black Power mandate or to protest the Vietnam War. He needn't have traveled to college campuses to advocate for African-American studies programs and an end to discriminatory employment practices. He was not obligated to serve others first as a leader of the movement, then as a public servant and finally as an educator. His career as an agitator for change was challenged at every step of the way. He was derailed repeatedly, and he repeatedly forced the heavy train of justice back onto the tracks. This was no easy life he had chosen.

But once you know a thing, and recognize its tyranny, you are left with a stark choice: to accept it or fight it. The latter comes with every uncertainty and danger imaginable. It is remarkable, therefore, that so many hundreds of civil rights activists and their supporters found ways to cause such a radical political and legal shift in the country. It is extraordinary that Sellers survived the ordeal and managed to do so much good despite brutal opposition. But Sellers and his fellow freedom fighters, though they tried as they might, could not manage to change the socio-economic realities of a nation that in the 50 years since Martin Luther King's assassination has experienced ever-worsening wealth, health and educational disparities, as well as an exploding prison population, especially among black males. This is the ever-current civil rights battle: to vanquish those forces that use poverty as a weapon for keeping African Americans and others disempowered. This is the battle younger generations of Americans have inherited from the justice warriors of Sellers' generation.

Driving through Denmark, Sellers is all smiles, waving at other drivers and pedestrians, rolling down the car window to chat with an acquaintance. He passes the rusty row of retail shops downtown, the old neighborhoods that once housed the proud, vital people of this small town. Sellers remembers his youth, his family, his childhood home to which he returned so many years later, after turmoil in Orangeburg and exile in Greensboro. He considers the challenges such places face, and the importance of black institutions such as Voorhees College. He finds some consolation knowing that his son Bakari is running ahead with the baton of social justice firmly in his grasp. He inflates with pride over Nosizwe's successes as a doctor and the pastoral work of his eldest child, Cleveland Lumumba Sellers III.

This small town reverberates with the voices and activities of a lost era. Everywhere Sellers looks he sees the atrophied present and the troubled past in juxtaposition, an old cast of characters— the ghosts of Denmark—coming to life in the hazy sunshine. Denmark is not in great shape these days. The poverty remains stark, the young people are mostly gone, the passenger trains are extinct. Commerce along Carolina Highway is reduced to a trickle.

But it's home. Sellers is home.

EPILOGUE

LATELY, IT HAS BEEN fashionable to ask the aging leaders of the civil rights movement to comment on current events. We know, more or less, what we want them to say. We want them to complain about how the pendulum has swung back in the other direction; how the gains they achieved have been eroded, often severely, by malicious government policies that sustain or exacerbate economic and social inequities; how American exceptionalism largely has been revealed a sham, at least for black people; how the long arc of the moral universe does not always bend toward justice. We expect them to repeat the cliché: "We've come a long way, but there's still a long way to go."

Cleveland Sellers, now in his 70s and still living in Denmark
50 years after the Orangeburg Massacre, did more than most to
force progress in the United States, but he is not deceived by the
uneven trajectory of the moral universe's arc. He is not fooled by
the romantic notion that all injustice might one day be resolved.
He knows who he is: a black man nearing the end of a productive
life replete with trauma and struggle whose great achievement has
been to assert his essential humanity in the face of powers designed
to erase it. Within that achievement are many smaller successes.
Sellers was one of hundreds of front-line civil rights activists who
captured the imagination of progressive-minded Americans and
arrested the attention of elected officials, influencing public policy
and breaking, finally, the strong grip of state-sanctioned racism.
Since 1968, public officials, with backing from intransigent voters and funders unable or unwilling to relinquish their bigotry,
have worked diligently to roll back the gains of the civil rights
movement and to define it in too-narrow terms as an enterprise
that addressed only racial inequity. Conveniently, those who cling
nostalgically to expired notions of inclusiveness fail to appreciate
the full scope of the movement, the many ways in which it confronted not only anti-black racism but economic disparities, unfair
labor practices, neo-colonialism, the horrors of the Vietnam War,
the oppression of Palestinians, apartheid in South Africa, Puerto
Rican self-determination, the plight of indigenous Americans,
black identity politics and the philosophies of Gandhi, Camus,
Nietzsche, Marx, Gramsci and others. Malcolm X became truly
dangerous not when he was berating the "white devil," but when,
near the end of his life, he began to embrace whites as brothers and
sisters in the greater cause for justice, when he understood that
all races shared a common enemy: a *system* of oppression. Martin
Luther King Jr. became truly dangerous not when he was leading
marches in the South and calling for black enfranchisement, but

when he turned his attention to poverty, housing discrimination and the Vietnam War. For it was with the Poor People's Campaign that King insisted on addressing the causes, and not merely the symptoms, of American social dysfunction and, in turn, threatened the foundational status quo of modern American capitalism itself.

"People are not satisfied where we are, but they are satisfied with what we did," Sellers said, arguing that the activists of the 1950s and 1960s too often don't take enough credit for their accomplishments. "Victories are victories, no matter how small." And therein lies an important idea: When you break down one wall in a series of walls, you enlarge the space within which you fight for justice. This space is occupied by opposing forces, and those forces might succeed in pushing you back to the rubble of the wall you shattered, or even further than that, but they will not likely succeed in rebuilding the wall. And even if they do, they will almost certainly rebuild it in a haphazard way, with weak areas made vulnerable by Supreme Court decisions, moral advancement, lived experience and a variety of other precedents. Sooner or later, you will push forward again and break down the next wall. This is what motivates Cleveland Sellers. This is what most black activists know. Resurgent white nationalism might shock many white people forced to see it close-up, but like all forms of social disease, when white supremacy doesn't find ways to infect the culture, it lies ever ready beneath the surface of social propriety.

Some of these lessons, along with the mantel of political activism, have been passed from father to son. Bakari Sellers has continued this multi-generational fight for justice first by becoming the youngest state representative in the history of South Carolina, by earning a law degree from the University of South Carolina and going to bat for underprivileged clients in court, and then by becoming a CNN commentator representing the Democratic Party, the 2016 Hillary Clinton campaign and other interests. He is certainly indebted to his father, and he knows it. Bakari Sellers often pays tribute to the elder activist and accompanies him to a variety of events. At Orangeburg Massacre commemorations, it becomes evident how the injuries inflicted by civil rights activism can be shared across generations.

Of all the many difficult confrontations Sellers faced over the years—the sit-ins; March on Washington; protest in Cambridge, Maryland; Freedom Summer 1964 and Atlantic City Democratic Party Convention; the Selma and Meredith Marches; SNCC in-fighting; anti-apartheid and anti-Vietnam War protests; FBI blacklisting—it was Orangeburg that left the deepest emotional wounds. "[In 1964], we asked people to go into harm's way," Cleveland Sellers said. "That's a different level of responsibility and one that's most difficult, because you ask somebody to go register to vote you can say that 'I will be there with you,' but you can't be with them 24/7, and you know that they'll probably lose their job, they'll probably lose the house they're living in, they probably could have somebody come by and shoot up the place, they could be arrested, they could even be killed—and that includes their children. We had to put on big-boy and big-girl pants at that particular time. It was a heck of a responsibility to take on." Assuming such responsibility, however daunting, forces one to grow up, to empathize with others, to strive to do the right thing.

But what happens when something goes wrong through no fault of your own and responsibility is assigned to you by your oppressors? What emotional havoc does that wreak? How did Sellers and others searching for three missing colleagues in July 1964 feel? What goes through one's mind when, despite long discussions, intense training sessions, network-building and strategizing, someone is hurt or killed? Who is to blame? What happens when, already coping with self-doubt and worry for others, you see your oppressor pointing his finger at you and announcing, *That's the person who got those kids killed at South Carolina State?* "That's the most damning thing that anybody could ever say to you because never was that a part of your overall objective and goals," Sellers said. "You have to be able to weather the storm on that one. The state did that for a long time, make victims the culprits."

IT HAS BEEN A STRUGGLE for him to weather that storm. All these years later, Sellers still cries when he thinks of the loss of life, the lingering blame and scapegoating, the miscarriage of justice, the refusal of the state to order an independent investigation of the incident and the relative historical obscurity of the Orangeburg Massacre. The wounds are not healed. The pain is handed down to a new generation, one coping with similar injustice in the form of militarized urban police forces often too eager to use their weapons on unarmed black boys and men. The laws have changed since Jim Crow, but in many ways not much has improved for the poor and disenfranchised. Here's what John Ehrlichman, counsel and assistant to the president for domestic affairs under Richard Nixon said about the "War on Drugs" launched by Nixon in the late 1960s:

> "The Nixon campaign in 1968, and the Nixon White House after that, had two enemies: the antiwar left and black people....We knew we couldn't make it illegal to be either against the war or black, but by getting the public to associate the hippies with marijuana and blacks with heroin, and then criminalizing both heavily, we could disrupt those communities. We could arrest their leaders, raid their homes, break up their meetings, and vilify them night after night on the evening news. Did we know we were lying about the drugs? Of course we did."

Sellers often refers to the so-called War on Drugs as an example of the government's deliberate, ongoing assault on black people. It's proof that there remains much work to do.

"You could actually see a correlation between high political consciousness and drug activity in [black] communities," Sellers remarked, saying he believes drugs were ushered in as a way to put black citizens behind bars. "That was one of the things that was very noticeable early on....It's hard not to interpret that as a deliberate attack." Sellers said that by the late 1960s, he and his colleagues felt as though they were always on the run, that their lives were imperiled, that time was running out to deliver their message. "We knew that the end was close," and after King's assassination, it seemed evident that SNCC's demise was just around the corner, he said. And soon enough, heroin was appearing in poor black neighborhoods. Then crack cocaine. And then young, poor black males were being demonized. And then the drug war contributed to mass incarceration and an increase in single moms and a cycle of desolate poverty that was harder than ever to break. "It just almost destroyed us completely," Sellers said of the crack epidemic. "It was devastating."

Mass incarceration is arguably one of two primary institutional obstacles that stand in the way of black self-determination and economic success today. The other is a deeply flawed public education system which has become more segregated in 2018 than it was in the late 1960s. It's difficult to tell the difference between school "reformers" and those who seek merely to privatize American education. Today, vouchers and other schemes that weaken public schools are being pushed harder than ever. The results are dubious. On average, it's been shown that charter schools enjoy less accountability and perform no better than their public-school counterparts. The effect of sanctioned "school choice" is to worsen the achievement gap between privileged and

underprivileged kids, to reduce available resources for traditional
public schools and drain them of talented students who opt to
attend a better-performing school elsewhere and to compound the
problem of racial and socio-economic segregation. This approach
has a disproportionately corrosive effect on minority families,
which has not gone unnoticed by Sellers and other veterans of the
civil rights movement.

Sellers has responded to all this with a sober combination of
distress and determination, focusing his efforts to combat these
destructive forces through education. Ever the mild-mannered
agitator, he has sought patiently to enlighten college students,
explain the accomplishments and failures of the civil rights movement, draw lessons from his own experiences and push ever forward. Even now, as he copes with a weakened heart that limits
his activity and a recent diagnosis of prostate cancer, Sellers is
agitating for change. He will appear at important public gather-
ings, offer an occasional interview, address college students. He
will tell them about all the "heroes and sheroes" of the movement,
the many people who risked their lives to push the boulder up the
hill a few more inches. He will tell them to learn their history, to
respect one another, to work together to affect change.

When Martin Luther King Jr. received his Nobel Peace Prize in
Oslo, Norway, on December 10, 1964, he deliberately gave credit
to the movement at-large in his speech: "I accept the Nobel Prize
for Peace at a moment when 22 million Negroes of the United
States of America are engaged in a creative battle to end the long
night of racial injustice," he said. "I accept this award on behalf of
a civil rights movement which is moving with determination and a
majestic scorn for risk and danger to establish a reign of freedom
and a rule of justice."

These words are music to Sellers' ears. "It is the movement
from which Dr. King emerges rather than the movement that

emerges from Dr. King," he once told a gathering in Charleston, South Carolina. The movement was not the invention of one man, nor did it start with Sellers' generation. His crusade is part of a long continuum of struggle that began centuries ago, when the first iron shackle was locked around the first black ankle in Africa. Really, it began before that. It began at the dawn of civilization, for tyranny is an integral part of the human experience, as is the fight against it.

Cleveland Sellers Jr. has done his part.

ACKNOWLEDGEMENTS

IT'S HARD TO WRITE A BOOK. It's an undertaking that requires months, even years, of preparation and research and interviews, purposeful and serendipitous encounters, lots of planning and thinking and talking, some luck, good editing and no small measure of encouragement.

I received such encouragement from a number of important people, each of whom can claim a piece of this biography. My wife, Giovanna De Luca, offered plenty of prodding, which sometimes came in the form of deserved chastisement. "Finish the book!" she'd say. "Stop wasting time!" My daughter, Zoë Alessandra, finally threatened me with a steep fine if I busted her deadline.

My colleagues at The Post and Courier provided essential if indirect support by permitting me to write semi-regularly about race, civil rights history, social justice and other issues, all relevant in various ways to the topic of this book. Indeed, the biography got its start as a four-part profile published in the newspaper in September 2008.

Jack Bass, a friend and mentor who covered the Orangeburg Massacre in 1968 for The Charlotte Observer and who has been one of Cleveland Sellers' staunchest defenders, was the one who first suggested that I write the newspaper profile and then provided welcomed support as I slogged my way through the research and writing of this volume.

The Rev. Joe Darby has always been happy to answer my queries about South Carolina history and politics, religious traditions and race relations, offering lucid insights (often with a twinkle in his eye and the suggestion of a smile on his lips) that I have absorbed with a keen ear and open mind. What's more, he has trusted me to write, on numerous occasions, the epic story of the African-American experience in the South.

Others offered invaluable assistance, especially some of the veterans of the civil rights movement whom I had the honor to meet over the years: Bob Zellner, Dorothy Zellner, Julian Bond, Judy Richardson, Nelson Johnson, Bill Saunders, John Lewis, Bob Moses, Howard Moore and Matthew Perry. They all replied graciously to my requests for interviews, and then generously enlightened an eager student of the civil rights movement who surely asked a few silly questions along the way.

I was thrilled to receive, late in the process, enthusiastic support from Hub City Press, a remarkable enterprise based in Spartanburg, South Carolina. Hub City has become a vital force, not just in the Southeast but nationally, publishing excellent volumes of fiction and nonfiction and securing a hard-won niche in the publishing world. When approached about issuing this biography, Betsy Teter embraced the opportunity then pushed me with excellent edits to craft a better book.

Most of all, it was the support I received from Cleveland Sellers himself that proved so essential. He put himself at my disposal again and again, patiently answering a slew of queries with the dispassionate brilliance of a true intellectual.

Sellers, I don't mind asserting, is an unusually kind and thoughtful man within whom the blue flame remains lit. He is not one to tolerate intolerance. I spent hours with him on many occasions, and each time felt enriched by the experience. I was learning a lot from someone modest and wise, a veteran of traumatic episodes that have left their scars but could not twist his gentle soul.

It happens that Sellers' life and character were informed largely by his determination to confront the long history of American racism, but one could imagine him in a different place and time confronting some other injustice, trying to set things right, patiently tutoring others. He is a truth-seeker, a freedom fighter, a family man and an educator. Cleveland Sellers Jr. is an earnest, imperfect human being who has strived to make the world a better place—for himself, to be sure, but mostly for all the rest of us, and for our children. For that, above all else, I thank him.

NOTES

CHAPTER 1 · CHILDHOOD IN DENMARK

Information on the Land Commission Program comes from *Promiseland: A Century of Life in a Negro Community*, Elizabeth Rauh Bethel (University of South Carolina Press, 1997 edition).

Descriptions of Denmark and of Sellers' family comes from the Papers of Cleveland Sellers Jr., Avery Research Center, College of Charleston; from *God's Long Summer: Stories of Faith and Civil Rights*, Charles Marsh (Princeton, 1997); and from interviews with Cleveland Sellers, Jim Campbell and Gwendolyn Sellers Parker.

Information about the role of northern Congregationalists in the formation of "normal" schools and other educational enterprises meant to serve blacks in the South comes from my article "Voyage to Freedom: Inspired by Amistad revolt, church sets course toward racial equality" (The Post and Courier, May 24, 2008); from *On the Heels of Freedom: The American Missionary Association's Bold Campaign to Educate Minds, Open Hearts, and Heal the Soul of a Divided Nation*, Joyce Hollyday (The Crossroad Publishing Company, 2005); from an interview with Hollyday; and from Voorhees College.

Information about Voorhees College founder Elizabeth Evelyn Wright comes from the article "History has missed the legacy of Voorhees College founder," Richard Reid, Feb. 10, 2009 (http://thetandd.com/news/history-has-missed-the-legacy-of-voorhees-college-founder/article_d4c41bd1-12d9-5971-adea-bb8fd64c7d83.html), and from *Elizabeth Evelyn Wright, 1872-1906: Founder of Voorhees College*, J. Kenneth Morris (University of the South, 1983).

The description of Sellers' Boy Scout experience comes, in part, from a National Public Radio report, Dec. 1, 2007, and from the article "Ex-Black Militant Becomes Eagle Scout," by Katrina Goggins of the Associated Press, Nov. 25, 2007.

CHAPTER 2 · GENERATIONAL DIVIDE

Details about the Emmett Till murder primarily comes from *A Death in the Delta: The Story of Emmett Till*, Stephen J. Whitfield (Johns Hopkins University Press, 1991) and from "The Shocking Story of Approved Killing in Mississippi," an article by William Bradford Huie appearing in Look magazine, January 1956.

The summary of Mack Charles Parker's killing is drawn from *Blood Justice: The Lynching of Mack Charles Parker*, Howard Smead (Oxford University Press, 1988).

Details about Sellers' childhood come from the collection of his papers at the Avery Research Center, College of Charleston, and from interviews with Sellers and Gwendolyn Sellers Parker.

Information about the Denmark sit-in comes from an article by E. Ashley Howell in Times and Democrat, Nov. 13, 2010, and from interviews with Sellers and Gwendolyn Sellers Parker.

Information about early unrest in Denmark, South Carolina, comes from *The River of No Return: The Autobiography of a Black Militant and the Life and Death of SNCC*, Cleveland Sellers with Robert Terrell (William Morrow and Company, 1973, reprinted by University of Mississippi Press in 1990).

Details about the NAACP's the Rev. Isaiah DeQuincey Newman comes from http://www.usca.edu/aasc/naacp.htm, Carol Sears Botsch and Robert E. Botsch, University of South Carolina-Aiken, 1997, and from an interview with Gwendolyn Sellers Parker.

The description of the Student Nonviolent Coordinating Committee comes from "SNCC: What We Did," by Julian Bond, published by Monthly Review Foundation, October 2000.

CHAPTER 3 · ENTER THE STUDENTS

The discussion of Sellers' experience at Howard University comes from interviews with Sellers, his memoir *The River of No Return* and from *Ready for Revolution: The Life and Struggles of Stokely Carmichael*, Stokely Carmichael with Ekwueme Michael Thelwell (Scribner, 2003).

The description of interactions with Malcolm X comes from interviews with Sellers.

Information about the debate between Malcolm X and Bayard Rustin comes from a video posted on YouTube, https://www.youtube.com/watch?v=eXUmCgEyyzs.

The fond words about Sellers and H. Rap Brown come from *Ready for Revolution*, Stokely Carmichael with Ekwueme Michael Thelwell (Scribner, 2003).

The reference to literacy tests in the Jim Crow South comes from *God's Long Summer*, Charles Marsh (Princeton, 1997).

The discussion of white supremacy tactics comes from *Defending White Democracy*, Jason Morgan Ward (University of North Carolina Press, 2014).

The long quote describing SCLC and the NAACP as old-fashioned and SNCC as an up-and-coming, action-oriented, grassroots civil rights organization comes from the article "SNCC: What We Did" by Julian Bond.

Information about Sellers early NAG and SNCC associations comes from his memoir *The River of No Return*.

Details about John Lewis' SNCC speech for the March on Washington, the controversy over it and what was cut from it, comes from Angus Johnston, http://studentactivism.net/2011/08/28/john-lewis/.

The discussion about King's role in the March on Washington, how he was perceived and how he benefited from the event, comes from Sellers' memoir *The River of No Return*.

CHAPTER 4 - INITIATION BY FIRE

Gloria Richardson's comment about the NAACP comes from, *African American Women's Rhetoric: The Search for Dignity, Personhood, and Honor*, Deborah F. Atwater (Lexington Books, 2009).

The description of the Cambridge Movement and street violence largely comes from *Civil War on Race Street: The Civil Rights Movement in Cambridge, Maryland*, Peter B. Levy (University Press of Florida, 2003), and from the article "Gloria Richardson and the Cambridge Movement" by Annette K. Brock, collected in *Women in the Civil Rights Movement: Trailblazers and Torchbearers* (Indiana University Press, 1993).

Additional information about the Cambridge Movement, Gloria Richardson and the street confrontations of 1963-64 comes from *Ready for Revolution* by Stokely Carmichael, from *The River of No Return* by Sellers, and from interviews with Sellers.

CHAPTER 5 - A TURNING POINT

The descriptions of the Mississippi Freedom Vote of 1963 comes from an interview with Sellers, from the Civil Rights in Mississippi Digital Archive, University of Southern Mississippi, from Marsh's *God's Long Summer*, and from Constance Curry's article "Mississippi History Now" (Mississippi Historical Society online newsletter).

Comments on preparations for Freedom Summer come from Carmichael's *Ready for Revolution*.

The description of the Mississippi Freedom Summer Project comes from several sources: interviews with Sellers; the documentary "Freedom on My Mind" in which Marshal Ganz is quoted; the website of the

University of Missouri-Kansas City Law School, http://law2.umkc.edu/
faculty/projects/ftrials/price&bowers/miss_chrono.html;   Sellers'   *The
River of No Return; Pillar of Fire: America in the King Years, 1963-65*, Taylor
Branch (Simon & Schuster, 1999); and Carmichael's *Ready for Revolution.*

The letter by Cleveland Sellers Sr. to his son comes from the papers of
Cleveland Sellers Jr., Avery Research Center, College of Charleston.

CHAPTER 6 · ATLANTIC CITY

Quotations of Bob Moses and Cleveland Sellers about the purpose of
the MFDP in Atlantic City, as well as descriptions of the confrontation
between the MFDP and Democratic Party officials and its significance,
come from Marshall Ganz's documentary "Freedom on My Mind," Clarity
Educational Productions (1994).

The audio and written transcript of Fannie Lou Hamer's testimony
before the Credentials Committee at the 1964 Democratic National
Convention comes from the American Public Media's American
RadioWorks website, http://americanradioworks.publicradio.org/fea-
tures/sayitplain/flhamer.html.

The "sick and tired" quotation of Hamer comes from *Race, Law and
American Society*, Gloria J. Browne-Marshall (Routledge, 2007).

Comments by H. Rap Brown come from his autobiography, "Die
Nigger Die!" which is available online at http://www.historyisaweapon.
com/defcon1/dnd.html#DIV9.

CHAPTER 7 · IN BETRAYAL'S WAKE

Information about Sellers and his family comes from interviews with
Sellers and from his memoir *The River of No Return.*

The description of Sellers' work in Holly Springs and the assessment
of the political situation, and opportunity, in Mississippi come from interviews with Sellers and from his memoir *The River of No Return.*

The description of the tension at SNCC's Waveland meeting comes from
"My Enduring 'Circle of Trust,'" an essay by Judy Richardson appearing

in *Hands on the Freedom Plow: Personal Accounts by Women in SNCC*, edited by Faith S. Holsaert, Martha Prescod Norman Noonan, Judy Richardson, Betty Garman Robinson, Jean Smith Young and Dorothy M. Zellner. Additional information comes from an interview with Dorothy Zellner.

The explanation of the Waveland meeting comes from *Many Minds, One Heart: SNCC's Dream for a New America*, Wesley C. Hogan (University of North Carolina Press, 2007).

Comments about SNCC strategy come from Sellers' *The River of No Return*. His recollection of Fannie Lou Hamer comes from an interview.

The outline of SNCC's four phases comes from Sellers' comments offered during a panel discussion at the SNCC 50th Anniversary Conference, Shaw University, Raleigh, N.C., April 15-18, 2010.

Reaction to Sellers' analysis of SNCC comes from an interview with Julian Bond.

Additional analysis of SNCC in 1965 comes from an interview with Bob Zellner.

Details about the Selma-Montgomery march come from *At Canaan's Edge: America in the King Years, 1965-68*, Taylor Branch (Simon & Schuster, 2006); *Pillar of Fire*, Taylor Branch (Touchstone/Simon & Schuster, 1998); an interview with Sellers for "Eyes on the Prize II" (Oct. 21, 1988); the Washington University Digital Gateway, http://digital.wustl.edu/e/eii/eiiweb/sel5427.0215.148clevelandsellers.html; *Taming the Storm: The Life and Times of Judge Frank M. Johnson Jr. and the South's Fight Over Civil Rights*, Jack Bass (Doubleday, 1993); and Sellers' *The River of No Return*.

Details about Malcolm X's visit to Selma and the impressions he made on SNCC and SCLC come from interviews with Sellers, from Branch's *At Canaan's Edge*, and from "Eyes on the Prize II." Sellers' reflections on the death of Malcolm X come from an interview.

CHAPTER 8 - BLACK POWER

The description of SNCC and the Lowndes County project comes from Sellers' *The River of No Return*; Carmichael's *Ready for Revolution*; *In*

Struggle: SNCC and the Black Awakening of the 1960s, Clayborne Carson (Harvard, 1981); and interviews with Sellers, Bob Zellner and Dottie Zellner.

The discussion of Black Power and its significance comes in part from my 2012 article "Black Power and its impact topic of Avery conference," appearing in *The (Charleston) Post and Courier*.

More on Black Power comes from *Dark Days, Bright Nights*, Peniel E. Joseph (Basic Civitas Books, 2010), and from *Where Do We Go From Here?*, Martin Luther King Jr., appearing in *A Testament of Hope: The Essential Writings and Speeches of Martin Luther King Jr.*, edited by James M. Washington (HarperCollins, 1986).

The discussion of Malcolm X in the context of Black Power comes from *Malcolm X: A Life of Reinvention*, Manning Marable (Viking Penguin, 2011).

The description of SNCC in transition in 1965 comes from Carson's *In Struggle*; from materials in Sellers' collection of papers at the Avery Research Center, College of Charleston; from Sellers' *The River of No Return*; and from interviews with Sellers, Bond and the Zellners.

CHAPTER 9 - IN CHARGE

The description of divisions within SNCC and the 1965 election comes from interviews with Sellers, his *The River of No Return*, Branch's *At Canaan's Edge* and interviews with Bob Zellner and Dorothy Zellner.

The quotes and description concerning SNCC's position on the Vietnam War come from "SNCC Statement on Vietnam," January 6, 1966, found in the Sellers' papers, Avery Research Center, College of Charleston.

Descriptions of the inner workings of SNCC and Sellers' role, as well as his views of Black Power, come from interviews with Sellers.

Information about the Atlanta Project comes from Carson's *In Struggle*.

Comments about SNCC's Nashville election come from an interview with John Lewis.

Information about Carmichael's rise in the ranks of SNCC and of Black

Power comes from an interview with Sellers, from Carson's *In Struggle* and from *Stokely: A Life*, Peniel E. Joseph (Basic Civitas, 2014).

CHAPTER 10 - REFUSING THE DRAFT

Stokely Carmichael's comments about his inability to join Sellers and Ruby Doris in the trenches comes from his *Ready for Revolution*.

The description of Carmichael's Black Power rhetoric and strategy comes from *New Day in Babylon*, William L. Van Deburg (University of Chicago Press, 1992).

Information about the FBI's views and observation of Carmichael and Sellers comes from Sellers' FBI file, declassified Jan. 15, 2008.

Details about Sellers' refusal to go to Vietnam comes from the SNCC newsletter of March 15, 1967, and other documents contained in Sellers private papers, Avery Research Center, College of Charleston, and from an interview with attorney Howard Moore.

CHAPTER 11 - UNDER FIRE

Information about SNCC's interest in various political movements of the time comes from interviews with Sellers; from his papers at the Avery Research Center, College of Charleston; from an interview with Dorothy Zellner; and from publications such as Joseph's *Stokely: A Life*, Carmichael's *Ready for Revolution*, and Carson's *In Struggle*.

Details about his relationship with Sandy Duncan, and his interest in going to S.C. State College to promote the idea of black studies, comes from interviews with Sellers.

The account of the first encounter between Jack Bass and Cleve Sellers comes from an interview with Jack Bass.

The description of the 1968 Orangeburg protests and campus shooting comes from interviews with Sellers; interviews with William Hine; interviews with Jack Bass; an interview with Jack McCray; and especially from *The Orangeburg Massacre*, Jack Bass and Jack Nelson (Mercer, 2002).

CHAPTER 12 - LEGAL WRANGLING, SNCC CHAOS

The assessment of Carmichael, Rap Brown and SNCC comes from a Department of Defense counter-intelligence report from 1967, available at http://www.aavw.org/protest/carmichael_sncc_abstract06_full.html

The derogatory reference to Sellers by Henry Lake comes from *The Orangeburg Massacre* by Bass and Nelson.

The reference to Martin Luther King Jr.'s response to the Orangeburg Massacre comes from *At Canaan's Edge* by Taylor Branch.

The description of the aftermath of King's assassination in Washington, D.C., comes from Carmichael's *Ready for Revolution*, and from an interview with Sellers.

Information about the proposed merger between SNCC and the Black Panthers, and resistance to the idea, comes from the article "SNCC Crippled by Defection of Carmichael," Washington Post news service (published in the St. Petersburg Times), September 26, 1968.

Details about Sellers' marriage to Sandy Duncan comes from an interview with Sellers and from a marriage certificate.

Information about SNCC's internationalist focus, support of revolutionary movements and resulting controversies back home, come from an interview with Dorothy Zellner; an interview with Cleveland Sellers: and the papers of Cleveland Sellers Jr., Avery Research Center, College of Charleston.

Details about Sellers' last confrontations with SNCC affiliates comes from an interview with him.

CHAPTER 13 - THE TRIALS

Sellers' views on the Orangeburg Massacre, and his concerns about being targeted, come from a letter Sellers addressed to Gov. Robert McNair, Oct. 5, 2001, one of a few he sent over the course of several years.

Sellers' defiant statements after the Orangeburg Massacre come from an article by Sam E. McCuen published in The State newspaper (Columbia, S.C.), a clipping of which is among the papers of Cleveland Sellers Jr. at the Avery Research Center.

The remarks of Matthew Perry come from an interview conducted for a 2008 profile of Sellers published in The Post and Courier.

Details about the state troopers trial come mostly from *The Orangeburg Massacre* by Bass and Nelson, and from the Sellers' papers at the Avery Research Center.

Details about the legal case against Sellers, and the description of Circuit Court Judge John Grimball's decision, come from *The Orangeburg Massacre*, Bass and Nelson, from interviews with Howard Moore, Sellers and Bass and from news reports in The Times & Democrat.

Information about Gov. Robert McNair's political ambitions comes from his obituary, "Robert McNair, Governor of South Carolina in the '60s, Dies at 83," Jack Bass, *The New York Times*, Nov. 24, 2007.

Bakari Sellers' comments on the Orangeburg Massacre come from a video interview conducted by Julian Bond, available at https://www.youtube.com/watch?v=_7j_Q8KcTdc.

CHAPTER 14 - ENTERING A NEW LIFE

Details about Sellers' afro-centric interests, difficulty returning to South Carolina, and Harvard experiences come from interviews with Sellers.

Information about the civil rights struggle in Greensboro, N.C., and about some of the major figures on the front lines of that struggle, comes from *Civilities and Civil Rights: Greensboro, North Carolina, and the Black Struggle for Freedom*, William Chafe.

Additional information about Sellers' feelings about and activism in the civil rights movement in Greensboro comes from interviews with Sellers and an interview with Howard Fuller.

Details about campus activism in Greensboro and the formation of SOBU come from an interview with Howard Fuller; the papers of Cleveland Sellers Jr., Avery Research Center; an interview with Nelson Johnson and Lewis Brandon and Chafe's *Civilities and Civil Rights*.

Information about SOBU the Voorhees rebellion comes from interviews

with Sellers and Leila Potts-Campbell and from Sellers' papers at the
Avery Research Center.

CHAPTER 15 · OFF TO PRISON

The description of the 1969 Greensboro Uprising at North Carolina
A&T University comes from Chafe's *Civilities and Civil Rights* and from
interviews with Sellers, Nelson Johnson and Lewis Brandon.

Details about Malcolm X Liberation University comes from the papers
of Cleveland Sellers Jr., Avery Research Center.

Details about Gwen Williamson and her relationship with Sellers come
from an interview with Sellers.

Details about Sellers' experience in prison come from an interview with
Sellers and from his papers at the Avery Research Center.

Additional information about Malcolm X Liberation University and its
founder Howard Fuller comes from interviews with Sellers; from the article
"Who is Howard Fuller and What Does He Want?" by Tom Bamberger,
Milwaukee Magazine, July 1988; and from the papers of Sellers, Avery
Research Center.

Details about Sellers' early efforts to find a job in Greensboro come
from an interview with Sellers.

Information about Sonja Haynes Stone comes from the article "Stone
is tenured," Black Ink student newspaper, University of North Carolina at
Chapel Hill, Aug. 18, 1980, and from an interview with Sellers.

CHAPTER 16 · GAINING TRACTION IN GREENSBORO

Details about the November 1979 "Death to the Klan" march in Greensboro
come from the Greensboro Truth and Reconciliation Commission Final
Report, Chapter 7, "Sequence of events on Nov. 3, 1979" (May 25, 2006);
from the Associated Press article "Anti-Klan marchers demonstrate peacefully," appearing in The Lakeland Ledger (Fla.), Feb. 3, 1980; and from
interviews with Sellers and Johnson.

Information about Sellers' campaign for Greensboro city council comes from *Once Upon a City: Greensboro, North Carolina's Second Century*, Howard E. Covington Jr., Joseph M. Bryan Foundation of Greater Greensboro, Inc. (2014); from interviews with Sellers; and from *The River of No Return*.

Descriptions of Sellers' work for the presidential campaign of Jesse Jackson come from interviews with Sellers and Jackson, and from Sellers papers at the Avery Research Center.

Details about family life in Greensboro come from interviews with Cleveland Sellers Jr., Nosizwe Sellers and Bakari Sellers.

CHAPTER 17 · PARDONED

Details about Sellers' parents, and his mother's cancer, come from an interview with Sellers.

The description of Sellers' pardon comes from an interview with Jack Bass.

The quote from The State newspaper July 25, 1993 editorial about Sellers' pardon comes from the article "Justice Finally Comes in the Orangeburg Massacre," Jack Bass in the Los Angeles Times, August 22, 1993. Sellers' reflections on the pardon come from an interview.

The comment from McNair about Sellers comes from the "Governor McNair Oral History Project" by the South Carolina Department of Archives and History, led by interviewer Cole Blease Graham (August 23, 1983). See http://library.sc.edu/file/1857.

Information about Robert McNair's attitude toward Sellers and his opinion of what happened at S.C. State College on Feb. 8, 1968, comes from a letter from Jack Bass to McNair, Feb. 27, 2007, and from letters from Sellers to McNair, Dec. 4, 1996; May 4, 2000; Oct. 5, 2001.

CHAPTER 18 · WITHIN THE ESTABLISHMENT

Comments from University of South Carolina President Harris Pastides come from an interview.

Details about Sellers' experiences in the African-American Studies program at the University of South Carolina come from interviews with Val

Littlefield, director of African-American Studies at USC; Kent Germany and Kim Simmons, professors in the program; and Sellers.

The detail about Carl B. Stokes at the University of South Carolina comes from an interview with Sellers.

Information about Sellers' mentorship of Jodie Walker comes from an interview with Sellers.

The discussion with Andrew Sorensen about race relations in Columbia, HBCUs and black studies comes from an interview with Sorenson.

CHAPTER 19 - CLOSING THE CIRCLE

The reference to former Voorhees College President Lee E. Monroe was drawn from the Orangeburg Times and Democrat article "Jury: Voorhees president sexually harassed professor; College failed to protect employee's rights, panel finds," April 27, 2007.

Information about life in Denmark and the obligations of the president come from interviews with Sellers, his former wife, Gwendolyn Sellers, and former Denmark Mayor Carrie Simmons.

Information about HBCUs and their historical and current role and status comes from essays by Walter E. Massey, president of Morehouse College, and by Norman C. Francis, president of Xavier University, collected in *The Future of Historically Black Colleges and Universities: Ten Presidents Speak Out*, edited by Carolyn O. Wilson Mbajekwe (McFarland & Company, 2006); from Part 4 of my 2008 profile of Sellers for The Post and Courier; from the article "How HBCUs can increase Alumni donation rates," Larisa Robinson, The HBCU Foundation (http://thehbcufoundation.org/how-hbcus-can-increase-alumni-donation-rates/); from the essay "The Changing Role of Historically Black Colleges and Universities: Vistas on Dual Missions, Desegregation, and Diversity," M. Christopher Brown II, Ronyelle Bertrand Ricard and Saran Donahoo, collected in *Black Colleges: New Perspectives on Policy and Practice*, edited by M. Christopher Brown II and Kassie Freeman (Praeger, 2004); and from the article "Historically black colleges challenged by economic hardships" by Sharon Sheridan, Episcopal News Service, Feb. 28, 2014 (http://episcopaldigitalnetwork.com/ens/2014/02/28/ historically-black-colleges-challenged-by-economic-hardships/).

Details about Sellers' tenure as president of Voorhees College come from interviews with Sellers.

CHAPTER 20 · INHERITANCE

Details about Sellers' health problems, private life and family come from interviews with Sellers and his son Bakari Sellers.

Information about Sellers' retirement from Voorhees College comes from an interview with Sellers and from the article "Sellers announces retirement as Voorhees president," The Times & Democrat, Sept. 17, 2015 (http://thetandd.com/news/standing-on-the-promises-mother-of-rep-sellers-continues-fight/article_1f0474c2-51aa-11e4-a48b-5be76717cf66. html).

EPILOGUE

Reflections on the civil rights movement come from interviews with Sellers.

Information about the so-called War on Drugs, comes from the article "Legalize It All," appearing in Harper's Magazine (https://harpers. org/archive/2016/04/legalize-it-all/), from Michelle Alexander's The New Jim Crow and from the work of the Children's Fund and the writings and speeches of Bryan Stevenson.

Information about the privatization of the education system and some of the outcomes of that effort come from a report available from the Civil Rights Project website at the University of California, Los Angeles (https://www.civilrightsproject.ucla.edu/research/k-12-educa-tion/integration-and-diversity/historic-reversals-accelerating-resegrega-tion-and-the-need-for-new-integration-strategies-1/orfield-historic-re-versals-accelerating.pdf); from the article "Charter schools perform no better, and often worse, than public schools," published by the National

Education   Association   (http://www.nea.org/home/32999.htm);   and
from the article "Charters not outperforming nation's traditional public
schools, report says," The Washington Post (https://www.washington-
post.com/local/education/charters-not-outperforming-nations-tradition-
al-public-schools-report-says/2013/06/24/23f19bb8-dd0c-11e2-bd83-
e99e43c336ed_story.html).

Sellers' reflections on the movement, delivered in a 2009 speech, come
from my article "Sellers recalls struggle," appearing in The Post and Courier
(http://www.postandcourier.com/news/sellers-recalls-struggle/article_
c843af40-e7ef-59b3-acff-b3f689a91d7d.html).

BIBLIOGRAPHY

BOOKS

Alexander, Michelle. 2012. *The New Jim Crow: Mass Incarceration in the Age of Colorblindness*. The New Press.

Atwater, Deborah F. 2009. *African American Women's Rhetoric: The Search for Dignity, Personhood, and Honor.* Lexington Books.

Bass, Jack. 1993. *Taming the Storm: The Life and Times of Judge Frank M. Johnson Jr. and the South's Fight Over Civil Rights*. Doubleday.

Bass, Jack and Nelson, Jack. 2002. *The Orangeburg Massacre*. Mercer University Press.

Bethel, Elizabeth Rauh. 1997. *Promiseland: A Century of Life in a Negro Community*. University of South Carolina Press.

Branch, Taylor. 1999. *Pillar of Fire: America in the King Years, 1963-65*. Simon & Schuster.

Branch, Taylor. 2006. *At Canaan's Edge: America in the King Years, 1965-68*. Simon & Schuster.

Black Colleges: New Perspectives on Policy and Practice. Edited by M. Christopher Brown II and Kassie Freeman. 2004. Praeger.

Browne-Marshall, Gloria J. 2007. *Race, Law and American Society*. Routledge.

Carmichael, Stokely, with Ekwueme Michael Thelwell. 2003. *Ready for Revolution: The Life and Struggles of Stokely Carmichael.* Scribner.

Carson, Clayborne. 1981. *In Struggle: SNCC and the Black Awakening of the 1960s.* Harvard University Press.

Chafe, William. 1980. *Civilities and Civil Rights: Greensboro, North Carolina, and the Black Struggle for Freedom.* Oxford University Press.

Covington Jr., Howard E. 2014. *Once Upon a City: Greensboro, North Carolina's Second Century.* Joseph M. Bryan Foundation of Greater Greensboro, Inc.

Women in the Civil Rights Movement: Trailblazers and Torchbearers. Edited by Vicki L. Crawford, Jacqueline Anne Rouse and Barbara Woods. 1993. Indiana University Press.

Genovese, Eugene D. 1976. *Roll, Jordan, Roll: The World the Slaves Made.* Vintage Books.

Hollyday, Joyce. 2005. *On the Heels of Freedom: The American Missionary Association's Bold Campaign to Educate Minds, Open Hearts, and Heal the Soul of a Divided Nation.* The Crossroad Publishing Company.

Hogan, Wesley C. 2007. *Many Minds, One Heart: SNCC's Dream for a New America.* University of North Carolina Press.

Hands on the Freedom Plow: Personal Accounts by Women in SNCC. Edited by Faith S. Holsaert, Martha Prescod Norman Noonan, Judy Richardson, Betty Garman Robinson, Jean Smith Young, Dorothy M. Zellner. 2010. University of Illinois Press.

Joseph, Peniel E. 2010. *Dark Days, Bright Nights.* Basic Civitas Books.

Joseph, Peniel E. 2014. *Stokely: A Life.* Basic Civitas Books.

Joyner, Charles. 1985. *Down by the Riverside: A South Carolina Slave Community.* University of Illinois Press.

Levy, Peter B. 2003. *Civil War on Race Street: The Civil Rights Movement in Cambridge,* Maryland. University Press of Florida.

Marable, Manning. 2011. *Malcolm X: A Life of Reinvention.* Viking Penguin.

Marsh, Charles. 1997. *God's Long Summer: Stories of Faith and Civil Rights.* Princeton University Press.

Toward the Meeting of the Waters: Currents in the Civil Rights Movement of South Carolina during the Twentieth Century. Editors Winfred B. Moore Jr. and Orville Vernon Burton. 2008. University of South Carolina Press.

Morris, J. Kenneth. 1983. *Elizabeth Evelyn Wright, 1872-1906: Founder of Voorhees College.* University of the South.

Raboteau, Albert J. 1978. *Slave Religion: The 'Invisible Institution' in the Antebellum South.* Oxford University Press.

Shuler, Jack. 2012. *Blood & Bone: Truth and Reconciliation in a Southern Town.* University of South Carolina Press.

Sellers, Cleveland, with Robert Terrell. 1973. *The River of No Return: The Autobiography of a Black Militant and the Life and Death of SNCC.* University of Mississippi Press.

Van Deburg, William L. 1992. *New Day in Babylon.* University of Chicago Press.

Ward, Jason Morgan. 2011. *Defending White Democracy.* University of North Carolina Press.

Whitfield, Stephen J. 1991. *A Death in the Delta: The Story of Emmett Till.* Johns Hopkins University Press.

The Future of Historically Black Colleges and Universities: Ten Presidents Speak Out. Edited by Carolyn O. Wilson Mbajekwe. 2006. McFarland & Company.

ARTICLES & REPORTS

"The Open Mind" (PBS), Feb. 10, 1957 interview on the topic of "The New Negro," with the Rev. Dr. Martin Luther King Jr. and Judge J. Waties Waring.

"The Shocking Story of Approved Killing in Mississippi" by William Bradford Huie, Look magazine, January 1956.

"Voyage to Freedom: Inspired by Amistad revolt, church sets course toward racial equality," Adam Parker, The Post and Courier, May 24, 2008.

National Public Radio report, Dec. 1, 2007; Katrina Goggins, "Ex-Black Militant Becomes Eagle Scout," Associated Press, Nov. 25, 2007.

"SNCC: What We Did," Julian Bond, Monthly Review Foundation, October 2000.

"Leading from the pulpit," Adam Parker, The Post and Courier, Nov. 28, 2010.

"They Changed the World: The Story of the Montgomery Bus Boycott," The Montgomery Advertiser.

"Mississippi History Now," Constance Curry, Mississippi Historical Society online newsletter, Feb. 2011.

"Black Power and its impact topic of Avery conference," Adam Parker, The Post and Courier, Sept. 16, 2012.

"A lifetime of change," Adam Parker, The Post and Courier, Sept. 2008.

"Robert McNair, Governor of South Carolina in the '60s, Dies at 83," Jack Bass, The New York Times, Nov. 24, 2007. (http://www.nytimes.com/2007/11/24/us/24mcnair.html).

"SNCC Crippled by Defection of Carmichael," Washington Post news service (St. Petersburg Times), September 26, 1968.

"Who is Howard Fuller and What Does He Want?" Tom Bamberger, Milwaukee Magazine, July 1988.

"Stone is tenured," Black Ink student newspaper, University of North Carolina at Chapel Hill, Aug. 18, 1980.

Greensboro Truth and Reconciliation Commission Final Report, Chapter 7, "Sequence of events on Nov. 3, 1979" (May 25, 2006).

"Anti-Klan marchers demonstrate peacefully," Associated Press in The Lakeland Ledger (Florida), Feb. 3, 1980.

"Justice Finally Comes in the Orangeburg Massacre," Jack Bass in the Los Angeles Times, August 22, 1993, citing editorial in The State newspaper, July 25, 1993.

"History has missed the legacy of Voorhees College founder," Richard Reid, The Times and Democrat, Feb. 10, 2009. (http://thetandd.com/

news/history-has-missed-the-legacy-of-voorhees-college-founder/
article_d4c41bd1-12d9-5971-adea-bb8fd64c7d83.html)

"Historically black colleges challenged by economic hardships," Sharon
Sheridan, Episcopal News Service, Feb. 28, 2014. (http://episcopaldigi-
talnetwork.com/ens/2014/02/28/historically-black-colleges-challenged
-by-economic-hardships/).

"Sellers announces retirement as Voorhees president," The Times &
Democrat, Sept. 17, 2015 (http://thetandd.com/news/standing-on-
the-promises-mother-of-rep-sellers-continues-fight/article_1f0474c2-
51aa-11e4-a48b-5be76717cf66.html).

"Sellers recalls struggle," Adam Parker, The Post and Courier, Jan. 14,
2009. (http://www.postandcourier.com/news/sellers-recalls-struggle/
article_c843af40-e7ef-59b3-acff-b3f689a91d7d.html).

INTERVIEWS

Jack Bass (2010)

Julian Bond (2010)

Lewis Brandon (2012)

Jim Campbell (2011)

Dave Dennis (2015)

Howard Fuller (2015)

Kent Germany (2010)

Nikki Giovanni (2011)

William Hine (2011)

Joyce Hollyday (2008)

Jesse Jackson (2010, 2016)

Nelson Johnson (2012)

John Lewis (2008)

Valinda Littlefield (2010)

Georgette Mayo (2011)

Jack McCray (2011)

Howard Moore (2010)

Bob Moses (2014)

Gwendolyn Sellers Parker (2011)

Leila Potts-Campbell (2011)

Judy Richardson (2010)

Bill Saunders (2015)

Bakari Sellers (2008, 2016)

Cleveland Sellers (2008, 2010, 2011, 2012, 2015, 2016, 2017, 2018)

Gwen Sellers (2008)

Nosizwe Sellers (2015)

Kim Simmons (2011)

Andrew Sorenson (2008)

Bob Zellner (2010)

Dorothy Zellner (2010)

INDEX

ABOUT THE AUTHOR

ADAM PARKER earned degrees in music, then spent a decade in the business world before going back to school to earn a graduate degree in journalism from Columbia University. He taught journalism as an adjunct professor at the College of Charleston and soon landed a job at *The Post and Courier*. At the newspaper, he worked as a copy editor, metro editor, general assignment reporter, restaurant critic and religion reporter, arts writer and more. A long-time student of the civil rights movement and race in America, he has written extensively about the African-American experience. *Outside Agitator* is his first book.

HUB CITY
PRESS

HUB CITY PRESS is a non-profit independent press in Spartanburg, SC that publishes well-crafted, high-quality works by new and established authors, with an emphasis on the Southern experience. We are committed to high-caliber novels, short stories, poetry, plays, memoir, and works emphasizing regional culture and history. We are particularly interested in books with a strong sense of place.

Hub City Press is an imprint of the non-profit Hub City Writers Project, founded in 1995 to foster a sense of community through the literary arts. Our metaphor of organization purposely looks backward to the nineteenth century when Spartanburg was known as the "hub city," a place where railroads converged and departed.

RECENT HUB CITY PRESS TITLES

Flight Path • Hannah Palmer

Wild South Carolina • Liesel and Susan Hamilton

Suburban Gospel • Mark Beaver

Turning Point • Katherine Cann

Janson Text LT Pro
11.2 / 16.2